T0304988

Expect nothing.
Step as the Everything
last. Personal best.
how you respond that matters.
Run Your Own Race.
we conquer but ourselves.
achieve. it's how
the body can you fall, Start small. many times
es big way. Strength in vulnerability There is
Back up. you get

by Adele & Roberta Kate Holderness and Audre

Personal Best

Personal Best

From Rock Bottom
to the Top of the world

Adele Roberts

with co-author Kate Holderness

First published in Great Britain in 2024 by Hodder Catalyst
An imprint of Hodder & Stoughton Limited
An Hachette UK company

1

Copyright © Adele Roberts 2024

The right of Adele Roberts to be identified as the Author of the Work has been
asserted by her in accordance with the Copyright, Designs and Patents Act 1988.

Co-author: Kate Holderness

All rights reserved. No part of this publication may be reproduced, stored
in a retrieval system, or transmitted, in any form or by any means without
the prior written permission of the publisher, nor be otherwise circulated
in any form of binding or cover other than that in which it is published and
without a similar condition being imposed on the subsequent purchaser.

A CIP catalogue record for this title is available from the British Library

Hardback ISBN 9781399732826
ebook ISBN 9781399732840

Typeset in Electra by Hewer Text UK Ltd
Printed and bound in Great Britain by Clays Ltd, Elcograf S.p.A.

Hodder & Stoughton policy is to use papers that are natural, renewable
and recyclable products and made from wood grown in sustainable
forests. The logging and manufacturing processes are expected to
conform to the environmental regulations of the country of origin.

Hodder Catalyst
Hodder & Stoughton Limited
Carmelite House
50 Victoria Embankment
London EC4Y 0DZ

www.hoddercatalyst.co.uk

Contents

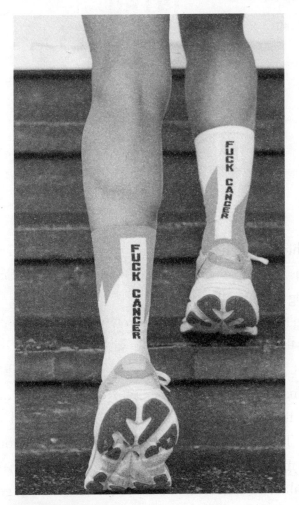

Step by Step
Whitney Houston

INTRO

'There's a road I have to follow.'

Step by Step

Eighteen months ago, I thought I was going to die; I thought I was a dead woman walking. Now, Ian Beale from *EastEnders* is eyeing up my waffles.

I don't blame him. They're currently poking out of the top of my see-through kit bag and, to be fair to Ian, they do look magnificent. A lovely pair of golden brown, Belgian-style waffles, individually packaged and ready to eat – *prêt à manger*. I'd stuffed them in my bag last night, thinking they'd come in handy. The breakfast of champions. Right now, though, I'm feeling more prêt à vommay – ready to be sick. I'm trying to act cool, calm and collected, like it's totally normal to be getting on a coach full of famous people. Our destination? The London Marathon. I feel like my whole world is about to fall out of my bottom, but then I remember that can't technically happen at the moment. I can't actually 'go' to the toilet anymore. My bum doesn't work . . . but more on that later.

For now, I try to act like a normal person on a normal coach and find a seat. One not too near the back so I don't seem like I'm going to be naughty and play tunes off my phone; one not too near the front so I don't seem like a square. I'm far from being a teenager anymore, but I seem to have regressed into school mode and my inner child is screaming. Sonia Fowler is on here somewhere. I think she's under one of those baseball caps near the front. I think Heather Peace is on here too. She's off *London's Burning*. OH MY GOD! This is amazing! Chris Evans (the radio one, not the superhero one) is at the front, titting about pretending to be our tour guide. He's nailing it. His voice is booming down the coach. I don't know if he's on the microphone or if he's just got a cracking pair of lungs, but the whole bus is filled with his big race day energy. I'm in Wonderland. I'm in my teenage dreams. I'm part star-struck, part terrified. Half of me feels like I'm on *Celebrity Coach Trip* and the other half like I'm being driven to my death. How is everyone so relaxed? So calm and happy? I'm absolutely bricking it! I'm trying to act normal, but I'm failing miserably. Kate, my girlfriend, is sitting next to me. I know she can sense my fear and she steps in to save me with some gentle small talk:

Kate: 'What did Adam say?'

Me: 'Who's Adam?'

Kate: 'Adam Woodyatt.'

Me: *looks at her blankly.*

Kate: 'Ian Beale . . .'

Me: 'Oh! He said he liked my waffles. So I said do you want one and he said no.'

She smiles at me with kindness, but I also sense a bit of pity in her eyes. My first failure of the day: I can't even give Ian Beale a waffle. And they're individually wrapped too.

As surreal as this moment is, it feels quite normal compared to the last 18 months. Even though I'm terrified, I'm so grateful to be here, on this coach, clutching my kit bag for dear life, next to the woman I love. In about three hours she'll guide me to the start line of the London Marathon and wave me off into the race of a lifetime.

Eighteen months ago I attended the London Marathon as a spectator, a supporter, a cheerleader, a DJ and, as I'd found out two days before, as someone with bowel cancer. I'll remember that marathon forever. The 3rd of October 2021. That one wasn't mine to run. I had the privilege of DJing at the race and cheering on and supporting the incredible runners. I remember being so present, really being aware of each person, screaming their names with everything I had and hoping they'd hear me. I felt so grateful to every single one of them and to every charity they were out there running for. They say that if you ever need to restore your faith in humanity, go to a marathon. The atmosphere is incredible – it's so special; strangers becoming friends and everyone thinking of and helping others. It was like medicine for me. My body was finding it hard by that point. It was shutting down. I remember having to wear sanitary pads because I was losing so much blood from my bottom. My tummy was bloated and my frame was small. But in that atmosphere, in that magic, I knew I'd be OK.

The human spirit is a powerful thing.

I had no guarantees at that marathon. I didn't know if I'd ever see another one. I certainly didn't know if I'd ever run one again.

3

But standing there that day, I knew I'd give it my all, whatever 'it' would turn out to be.

If you are already worrying that this book is going to be super sporty and marathony, fear not – yes, there are plenty of running bits in here to keep the Sporty Spices happy, but these chapters, they're really about life and how we make it through, even when we are not sure it is even possible; it's about that fighting spirit. The marathon serves as the perfect metaphor for the human experience. If you're reading this, you're in it – you're already making your way through the great marathon of life.

Everything that I'd been through had led me to this point. I was on the start line of one of life's marathons, with all its twists and turns, trials and tribulations, soaring highs and crushing lows. And even though the cancer had taken hold of my body, that was the most I was willing to allow. It would not take my spirit and it would not take my soul. As with most of us, this wasn't my first rodeo. I may not have faced cancer before, but I'd been 'through it' – because our lives are full of marathons and mountains to climb. Each of us has our own version of what that means to us.

So, whatever you're facing in life at the moment – if you're going through a tough time and you don't think you can go on, if you're looking to make a change, if you're ready to take that leap of faith, if you're about to face something you're not sure you can do – *this book is for you*. I hope it brings you comfort, companionship and, most of all, reminds you that you are not alone. Aside from that, I hope it's just a cool story! However this book found its way to you, I am so happy. I am super grateful it's in your hands. Thank you. I promise not to wang on too much or take up too much of your time, but I hope it adds value to your outlook when navigating the shit storms and rocky terrains of life. I also hope I don't come across as preachy or telling you how to live your life. This is merely a collection of things that happened *to me* that I hope can help somebody else, somewhere, in some way . . . because that's what others have done for me. The most valuable lesson that I've learned through all of this is that you can only try your best, and that's what this book is all about. We each possess our own unique personal best, and when we tap into that, we cannot be stopped. So hold on to your hats, kids, we're about to go on a bumpy ride!

Today is the 23rd of April 2023 – fewer than 18 months since I had life-saving surgery and less than a year since I finished chemotherapy. This is the story of those 18 months and the self-discovery, the realisations, the belief and the mindset that went into them. I didn't know it at the time, but I'd been training for this moment all my life, taking knock-backs and learning lessons that would crystallise at just the right time to get me through. So, I guess this is the story of me finally putting into practice the important lessons that life had been teaching me all along. This is also my tribute to every single person who has heard the words 'you have cancer'. To their loved ones, to their families and to their friends. You are not alone. This is a thank you to the incredible NHS. To all of the amazing runners who challenge themselves and run races to give back and help others. And if you're currently facing one of life's marathons, this is especially for you.

So how do you run a marathon? One – step – at – a – time.

And it's time.

It's time to run for my life!

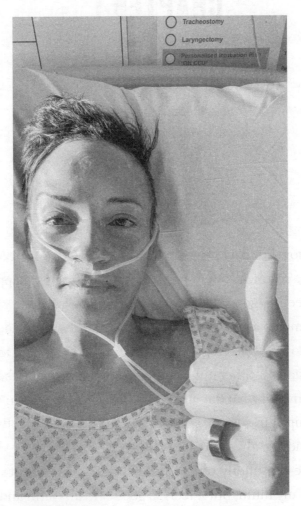

I Will Survive
Gloria Gaynor

CHAPTER 1

'Did you think I'd crumble?'

I Will Survive

And now I'm back, from outer space. What a magical, mystical, cosmical ride. I've got no idea what just happened, but I'm feeling good. Loosey-goosey. It takes a couple of minutes for my spaceship to land and its crew of one to earth. Re-entry to the atmosphere is wobbly, but I slowly begin to acclimatise. I start to gather my wits about me, working out who I am, where I am and what the hell I've just been through. I'm not on a spaceship, I'm just spaced out. I'm in the hospital. But I'm awake. And I'm alive! ME SO HAPPY!

I realise I'm utterly off my head. But it's all right, it's legal. Don't tell my mum, but it feels so good. I'm all warm and snuggly and spangly. I have arisen from my morphine dream and my intergalactic journey aboard the good ship NHS *Enterprise* is complete. The doctors have navigated into my abyss, probed my deep space and extracted Umbriel. I don't know if it's normal to name your tumour, but I did. I called it Umbriel. Actually, seeing that written down, I think I've answered my own question.

It's definitely NOT normal to name a cancerous tumour, is it? LOL. Anyway, I'd recently flown to Belfast to record an episode of *Celebrity Mastermind*, and my specialist subject was 'The Planets of the Solar System', which is how I came to learn that Umbriel is one of the moons orbiting the planet Uranus. It's known as 'the dark moon of Uranus', and so it became the name I gave to the dark tumour of MY anus. Yep . . . this has been a weird month. Let's take it back a bit . . .

Allow me to take you into the rabbit hole. Pinch, punch, first of the month (or 'white rabbits' as we say round my way). It's the 1st of October 2021.

'Adele Roberts?' My name was called. Kate and I stood up and into the vortex we went. The point of no return. Through the sliding door of fate. I would leave that room a very different person. On the surface I'd look exactly the same, but inside I'd be changed forever. We didn't know how important that meeting would be. We never know when these moments will arrive, do we? So always be ready . . . and wear nice underwear.

I've got an appointment at the hospital to get the results of my colonoscopy. I'd been noticing a bit of blood when I went to the toilet and something had just felt 'off' with my digestion for a few months. Around July of 2021 the symptoms became harder to ignore, so I made a GP appointment. They thought it was piles, but gave me a FIT (Faecal Immunochemical Test) to do at home, just in case. After the test, I received a call to confirm that they'd found traces of blood in my poo, so could I come in for a colonoscopy? *Yeah, sure.* I didn't really know what a colonoscopy was, but I was game. I was sent 'bowel prep' to do before my appointment. *Cool!* I always remember my Uncle Tony saying you should have a colonic done at least once in your life because there's probably food and waste in there that's been lurking for years. I asked him what a colonic was, and it sounded like they basically put a hosepipe up your bum. Erm . . . I think I'll pass. Imagine pressure washing your back passage and having a Happy Meal that you ate when you were seven come flying out.

A colonoscopy though? This sounded more like a posh wash with a camera. The bowel prep, which you drink rather than administer via hosepipe, would naturally cleanse my colon and make it squeaky clean, ready to get papped. Now that sounds much nicer. Count me in.

I arrived for my colonoscopy, bowel prep done, hospital gown on and a shot of sedation to make the whole experience more agreeable. I'm quite sensitive to medication so I was absolutely off my head. It was so weird getting to see the inside of my colon on the big screen. It was like watching *Honey, I Shrunk the Kids.* I was simultaneously the big, giant me and the mini version of me travelling through my own bowels. What a trip!

Today it's time to get the results. We weren't sure if Kate would be allowed in due to Covid, but we'd politely ask and hopefully she could be in the room with me. Kate's my little recording device. She remembers everything. She's an actress and she can pretty much retain any scene that we experience in life and perform it back to me verbatim. I looked forward to her performance of 'Adele's colonoscopy results' later when we got back home. So off we went up to the hospital. We got our masks at reception. Kate was allowed to accompany me and we waited for my name to be called.

We entered the room. There were two lovely nurses in there already, Ann and Maria. I recognised Ann from my colonoscopy. I remembered her having such a lovely way about her and a gorgeous Irish accent too – I could listen to her talk for days. There were two chairs set out for us against the wall to our right. Kate and I sat down and a couple of minutes later, a man, who can only be described as fabulous, sashayed his way around a makeshift cubicle curtain, pulled up a chair and sat facing me and Kate. Introducing the incredible Mr Bhan. He reminded me of a musketeer. He was so cheery and full of life. He had a proper swashbuckle about him – like he drank beer from golden goblets. I didn't know what he was going to say, but he had this immense 'I've got this' energy.

He gathered himself, his face softened as he leaned towards me and, with as much kindness as he could, he said, 'It's cancer.'

It took me a few seconds to register what he'd said. *Wait a minute. What? I think he just said I have cancer.* He carried on speaking, but I couldn't take in what he was saying. *I've got cancer? But . . . but I can't have cancer. I'm not ill . . . CANCER?*

'Am I going to die?' I asked. That was my first thought. I wanted to know how long I had left to live. I thought I was gone.

'No, we can do something. We can help you.'

A rush of emotion erupted out of me. I must have been holding my breath. I audibly exhaled. It felt like the whole of my being rushed out of my body and into the room. I mustered my next question.

'Is it my fault?' My voice cracked, I could barely get my words out. The emotion was starting to hit.

'No,' he said.

My eyes started to sting. Ann got me a tissue. I don't remember what happened next, but Kate tells me Mr Bhan said something along the lines of, 'Before I go any further, I just need to do some checks to know if we can operate.'

The next thing I knew, I was behind the cubicle curtain and on a hospital bed with instructions to remove my underwear. I was to lie on my left side and pull my knees up to my chest. I think my brain imploded. Kate said she kept hearing the nurses say, 'Lie on your left. On your left, Adele, no, your *left*.' I was so overwhelmed I didn't even know my left from my right. I couldn't move. My body was in some kind of rigor mortis-like stupor. It took them a good few goes to get me to assume the position – they had to physically roll me over themselves so that Mr Bhan could begin his assessment.

Mr Bhan was checking the position of my tumour. It was so low in my colon that it made it trickier to operate, but Mr Bhan was confident he could remove it. He also said something about maybe needing something called a stoma, but not to worry because it would help my bowel to heal from the operation. As far as they knew, I had stage 2 cancer, but they needed to do more tests. My tumour was right near the wall of my colon so it could possibly be stage 3. They wouldn't know for another week. He said more kind stuff, mentioned he'd see me soon with the results and to discuss surgery and, with that, he swashbuckled out of the room with his big musketeer energy. Onwards, I'm sure, to help somebody else in need.

It was all a whirlwind. I didn't know what to think. Essentially, I'd walked into a room, was told I had cancer, was plopped onto a bed and had a man I'd only just met pop his fingers up my bum. All in the space of five minutes. I only came in for test results!

Poor Kate. I hadn't even had a chance to look at her properly. I hoped she was OK. Ann and Maria sat down with us and spent what seemed like a good half an hour explaining the next steps and giving us lots of reading material to take home. They were amazing, so gentle and kind, and it felt like we could have stayed as long as we wanted. There were shit loads of leaflets and book-lets. All about cancer. I was grateful for the help, but I was also baffled and overwhelmed. I kept thinking, *They think I've got cancer. What's going on? I'm not ill. Also, they don't know what stage cancer it is, so what if they've got it wrong? Will I die? Is he blagging me just to be nice?* I had so many questions.

We eventually stood up, hugged and thanked the nurses, and made our way out of the hospital.

It's strange finding out you have cancer. It didn't feel like I might have expected it to. I almost didn't 'feel' at all. I was numb. Maybe it was shock? I couldn't believe it. I think part of me still doesn't believe it to this day. I didn't cry. I think I just tried to let the news sink in and I'd see how I felt later. Technically, noth-ing had changed. I walked out of the room *feeling* as healthy as when I'd walked in. The only difference was a bit of knowledge. It was also something I couldn't do anything about. I couldn't even tell my family because we had no idea what stage it was and what we were dealing with. I knew they'd ask questions and I wanted to have the answers for them. I didn't want their minds racing at all hours just like mine. So, until we knew more, I'd decided to keep it to myself. Only me, Kate and the hospital knew.

So, there we were, walking out of the hospital like zombies, looking the same but feeling totally different. We went into autopilot – survival mode.

'Hang on,' I said to Kate. 'I just need to nip into Aldi to get some chicken thighs.'

'Yeah,' said Kate, 'I need to post this parcel for Vinted.'

That's how it happens. Life doesn't stop – it's business as usual. There is no right time, it's never convenient. You just have to be ready to roll with it when the shit storm arrives I suppose. So, with that, we bought the chicken, posted the parcel and went back to our new messed-up normal. And, thinking about it, I never did get that performance from Kate of 'Adele's colonoscopy results'.

The Waiting Game

The words had been spoken aloud: 'You have cancer.' I wouldn't find out what stage it was and what my chances of survival were for another week, and I still had a running event to host, a London Marathon DJ set to do and a quick flight to Belfast to record *Celebrity Mastermind* for the BBC. Wow . . . if I didn't laugh I'd have cried. For now, though, I was 100 per cent sure I was someone living with cancer. I didn't need to wonder any-more. It was here. It existed. The devil was within me and uncloaking it seemed to send it into overdrive. I went from bleeding small amounts from my bottom to being unable to control my bowels. Sanitary pads became an everyday necessity to stem the flow. I couldn't leave the house without dark scarlet blood clots staining my clothes. It felt like, once I'd heard the diagnosis, my body just gave up and surrendered itself. I had the perpetual feeling of needing to go to the toilet as my muscles would instinctively try to expel the foreign body. If I pushed my rectal muscles hard enough, the tumour would protrude from my bottom. I could actually see it – a bloody mass of malignant tissue. It was disgusting, otherworldly, like the Demogorgon off *Stranger Things*. I'm not even kidding. It was just like the demon of Hawkins, a monster deep-rooted in the bowels of the town, growing for years in the darkness. Now that it had been detect-ed, unmasked, it was going on a rampage, destroying everything in its path. This was my alien, and it was killing me. It was eating into the walls of my colon, systematically destroying me, bit by bit, every day. The Demogorgon, the alien, the cancerous Trojan horse, the dark moon – Umbriel.

The days waiting to get this demon out of me felt like years. It was an everyday battle. I won some, Umbriel won some. Two days after my diagnosis, I was at the aforementioned marathon, supporting, cheering and DJing. After my DJ set, Kate and I started the walk home. My heart was so happy and full, and for the couple of hours or so that I was at the race, I forgot about everything. I was on top. My spirit was fired up. That's when the script flipped. It was like the classic horror movie trope, 'Just when you think you're safe . . .'

On the walk home, Umbriel decided to burst my happy bubble. My body was so small by that point that my clothes didn't quite fit me. It was getting harder to walk, but I made sure I kept myself going each day – not giving in. Kate knew I was struggling and intuitively slowed with me. She didn't let on, but she was pretty much walking at a snail's pace. I was like her little toddler and she had all the patience in the world. By then, it was normal for my tummy to feel like it had permanent butterflies. I didn't feel excited or nervous though. It was stingy, like static energy or pins and needles racing around my body. I didn't feel right. My bottom was doing its usual routine of trying to expel Umbriel. It was like the lower half of my body was always kind of trying to be sick to get rid of what it knew shouldn't be there. I was used to these bowel convulsions going on without anything actually 'happening' at the business end, but suddenly, on that slow walk, small, pebble-like bits of waste started falling out of my too-loose pants. I couldn't control it. I just stood there as it happened. Me, soiling myself in the middle of the street. I was so embarrassed. I stood there on the streets of London, a couple of blocks away from the crowds of the marathon, shitting myself and hoping nobody had noticed. I looked up at Kate. I knew she'd seen, but she didn't say a word. She looked at me in a way only she can. In a way I've since seen many times – a look of kindness, understanding, devoid of judgement and full of defiance. My tummy was hurting, my body was failing, but I felt a rush. *Fuck you, Umbriel*, I thought. I let the moment (and the poop) pass. I put one foot in front of the other and, with Kate by my side, I started to walk again.

University College London Hospital, 7th Floor, Bed 49

Less than a month later, the morphine is beginning to thaw and my fingers are twitching. Where is my phone? I've got to ring Kate. I've got to FaceTime her. I've got to tell her we made it!

I start to regain some kind of connection between my mind and my body as my senses begin to wake up. My eyes are darting, scanning the new space, trying to get my bearings. Everything seems so quiet and gentle, while at the same time clinical and practical. My ears kick in. I pick up the beeping pulse of the heart rate monitor to my left. Is that mine? *Cool.* I can't hear much else. Am I the only one here? It all seems like a little utopia. A VIP experience. A Boots Red Letter Day. My bed sheets are crisp and white; my cubicle curtain is purple at the side and blue at the front. I'm lucky enough to be positioned near a window, and even though the curtains are closed, the rays of the autumnal evening sun are still making their way through. Everything seems to glow. As I scan my little pod to look for my bag, I see a high-backed, pale-blue nursing chair to my right. I might just pop on that and have a look for . . . *Oh no you bloody won't!* I'm stuck to the bed. That's when I notice that I've got tubes coming out of me all over the place. WTF? I'm plumbed in. I'm like a Tube map. I can't even see where some of these end. What are they connected to? Has someone tied me down? Oh my God . . . am I in *The Matrix*?

'Excuse me . . . nurse? Hello? I think someone's accidentally tied me to the bed. Anyone? Have you got some scissors? I think I might need cutting out.'

I lift up my head to try to see what's going on. Rookie error. The drugs are definitely starting to wear off now because boy do I feel it – the most overwhelming stabbing pain in my stomach followed by a hot, throbbing sensation as I wince back onto my pillow. *JEEZ!* And that's when I remember – I've just had major surgery. I've been blown up, punctured in at least five places, had tubes put in and a tumour taken out. I think there might be a titanium ring in there somewhere now, part of my bum has been removed and, for the *pièce de résistance*, there's a good chance my small intestine is now poking out of a hole in my stomach. I might have a stoma.

If you've never heard of a stoma before – neither had I until a few weeks before my operation – it's basically an opening anywhere on the body. In my case, I'd been told that it could be an ileostomy, which meant my small intestine would be pulled out of a hole in my belly allowing me to go to the toilet in a bag rather than the loo. I know, I'm making it all sound SO fun. I say 'could be' because there was no guarantee I was getting one. It was a *maybe* type situation, with the surgeon making the decision during the operation. Before going into hospital, I'd signed a form to consent to the surgery. I treated that form like I treat most wordy paperwork – *yeah, whatevs*. It could have said anything. But you know, I trust the NHS. They're kind, aren't they? Do what you want, huns! Later, when I gave the form to a responsible adult (Kate), I found out that it not only said that I was up for a stoma if the doctor thought I needed one but also that one of the side effects of this surgery – a low anterior resection – was death. I'd just ticked it and gone *yeah, no probs*.

Now I know this sounds irresponsibly blasé of me, but this is how I deal with stuff. I don't worry about things until they're here. It had since been confirmed that I had stage 2 bowel cancer, so if I needed a stoma to make me better, GET IT IN THERE! Rip that rectum out and get that stoma in! Swap a tumour for a stoma? Sounds like a bargain! Seriously though, I just didn't give myself time to dwell on it. It was there to save my life. Yeah, a quick glance on Google suggested they might not be the prettiest of things – I mean, you wouldn't want one on your face – but it is what it is. I've got bigger fish to fry, like BEING ALIVE, so essentially I'm good with it.

I pulled back my white sheets to see if I'd been gifted a stoma. I was actually a little bit excited. Elaine, my stoma nurse who I'd met a few days earlier, was a genius. Elaine is a credit to the NHS. From the moment she met me, she used her nursey, witchy senses to pick up on my personality, my worries, my fears and my unique challenges, gently and with care. She was amazing. She patiently gave me and Kate a full stoma masterclass on what to expect if I got one and, by the time she'd finished with me, I was sold. She was so good I think even Kate wanted one! Thanks to Elaine, a lot of the hard work had been done. She'd helped prepare me mentally, beginning to wrap my head around having a stoma before I physically faced it. Everything she'd already talked me through was about to happen. I just had to chill in my hospital bed and let it play out.

So here we go. Under the covers. Yep. That's the badger. I've got a stoma. And it's in a see-through bag. It's brand new! Oh wow – look at that little belter. There it was. About two inches of pink small intestine that, until this morning, was inside my body. Now it had been cut in half, fashioned into a loop and was currently poking out of the right side of my stomach and finished with an array of stitches. AND I WASN'T DEAD! How bloody brilliant is that? If I could have stood up I would have given the surgery team a standing ovation. What a marvel. 'Modern medicine' guys! My insides weren't just out – they were 'out out'.

I was dying to look at it properly, but I couldn't sit up so I just had a horizontal, skewed view. Once I got my phone in my hand, I tried to go on a sightseeing mission, sending my phone down there and taking a load of photos so I could get a better look – flash most definitely on. I just hoped no one came in and caught me doing it; how do you explain that? I got some good shots, but because my body was such a wreck, I couldn't make out what was what. It looked like the local tip. I was a mess.

As I lay staring in awe at my newly rearranged innards, a nurse slipped through my cubicle curtains and officially welcomed me to University College London Hospital. She helped me make that first call to Kate, holding the phone to my ear. Both Kate and the lovely nurse had to endure my psychobabble. I don't remember much of that conversation. Kate confirms I was still off my face. I think I told her I loved her a thousand times. I also asked her to tell my mum, my dad, my brothers and my sisters that I loved them too, like I was at the Oscars. Apparently, I also kept banging on about someone called Emma and how I needed to thank her. She got so many shout-outs. We still don't know if Emma was my anaesthetist, a nurse, a cleaner or a figment of my imagination, but Emma, if you're reading this, thank you!

The nurse said that the next day I'd be getting out of bed and sitting in that high-backed chair. I imagined that the seat would usually be reserved for visiting family and friends. Not this time though – nobody was coming to see me. Thanks, Covid. It was a strange time. I didn't see anyone's faces for the week I was there. I couldn't even see the faces of the NHS angels who were saving me – they were half-covered with blue masks. But I could see their kind eyes, and I could hear the warmth in their voices. I felt so cared for and safe as I lay in my little bay.

The chair was just to my right, a few inches or so away from my bed. I was in bum-shuffling distance. If I wasn't full of holes, I could have rolled over, reached out and touched it. But I *was* full of holes, and hooked up to at least three machines. My body was tender, sore and horizontal. I couldn't imagine I'd be rolling or reaching anytime soon; I could barely sit up. My head was faring a bit better – it was at least trying. I could move my neck! I tried to focus on that small win. The nurse explained that it wasn't good to stay lying down for too long as it put me at a higher risk of fluid settling in my body and could lead to an infection. I took a deep, painful breath and nodded with my trusty head, my only moveable body part.

'I'll be ready,' I told her. No excuses. Tomorrow it was on. I was going to mount that chair like a good 'un. Let's do this.

I slept like a baby that night. I was exhausted. Before my

surgery, I'd been told that my body was about to go on a huge journey and that I needed to prepare well. Because of the tumour, my digestion and appetite had been suffering, so I was given high-density nutrition shakes to help me get the calories I needed to fuel me during the operation and recovery. The stress my body would be under in surgery, I was told, was equivalent to completing a marathon. Now you're talking my language – hearing that made me smile. Before my body started to fail, I loved to run. It was my mobile meditation – it balanced me and helped me cope with life. It was my medicine. Because of running, I felt fit, happy and free. In the days leading up to my surgery, though, I was weak, hurting and, like I said before, dying. But although I didn't know it at the time, I think the mention of a marathon was the start of something. The seed had been planted. My brain heard the word and let it go, but my subconscious took note and committed to it. I couldn't even imagine attempting 26.2 miles as I lay in that hospital bed, but somewhere deep down a spark had been lit.

But that's way off in the future. For now, getting into a pale-blue, high-backed chair is my marathon. This was the lesson life was teaching me today. It's all relative.

No matter what your struggle is, no matter how big or small your challenges seem, you can do it. It all matters. It all counts.

Some days, just getting out of bed and facing the world is your marathon and, to me, that can be just as mentally tough as the race itself – sometimes more challenging. Never fear failure, fear not trying. If you're not trying, that's when you're dying.

In that hospital bed, my biggest challenge was to fight through the pain, sit up in bed and get to that high-backed chair. But first I had to make sense of all the tubes and monitors. I did a quick tally of them. One was for wee. OK. One was for vitamins and general stuff to keep me alive. One was for drugs, and there was my see-through stoma bag for poop. Kate's got this little label maker thingy at home that she uses to write things like 'Pasta' on a transparent jar that quite obviously has pasta in it. I take the mick out of her for it, but right then, I wished I could have borrowed it so I could neatly label my tubes.

Take the first step. And then the next. That was my strategy. So, the next day I would clip my catheter onto one side of my nightie and the big bag of blood and fluid being drained out of my body onto the other side. I'd somehow move my aching, bloated, perforated body to the right side of my bed and then make the leap, with the help of the nurses, to the chair. We'd get to the top of that pale-blue mountain. I might not get a medal, but I'd be so proud and when it's done, I'll wake up the next day and start over again. All I could ask of myself was my best.

'The beginning is the most important part of the work.'
– Plato

At that very moment, when I was literally lying down, that was when I needed to choose to get back up. These are the moments that make us. These are the moments that lead to our greatest achievements. To me, it's in these quiet moments, these seemingly impossible personal moments, maybe the ones only you get to see – the moments when you feel like you can't go on, when you doubt yourself, when you're scared . . . but you do it anyway – that to me is where the real courage lies. When you don't know what fate has in store, but you commit anyway; when you're willing to lose – that's fucking brave.

Having cancer wasn't my setback. It was the start of my comeback. It snapped me into the present, it woke me up. Waking up in the hospital that day, I didn't know what fate had in store for me, but I was sending a message: to my body, to my heart and to my soul. I won't give up. I'd already decided. There was no room for doubt. I wouldn't lie back and let circumstance dictate my life. Time to leave, cancer . . . so, go on now, go. Walk out the door!

I didn't know it at the time, but my marathon training had already begun.

NOTE TO SELF:
THE FIRST STEP IS JUST AS IMPORTANT AS THE LAST.

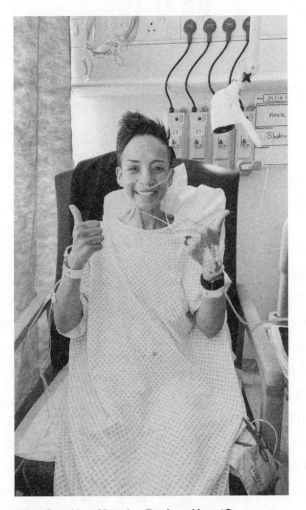

How Can You Mend a Broken Heart?
Al Green

CHAPTER 2

'How can you stop the rain from falling down?'

How Can You Mend a Broken Heart?

Veni, vidi, vici. I came, I saw, I conquered. A chair. A mountainous, pale-blue, high-backed chair. It might not be much to some, but to me it's a victory and I'll take the win. The immense sense of pride I felt after getting in that chair was incalculable. Physically it was a slight gesture, but mentally it was the signal I needed to galvanise every single cell in my body to take up arms and fight.

I don't know what it was about that ward, that hospital, whether it was the amazing NHS staff or the good fortune of being placed near the window, but I felt good. I got up every day with hope and a sense of adventure. I mean the drugs and the removal of a murderous tumour might have helped a bit, but I'd never been happier. I felt like I was getting my life back. Like a curse had been lifted. I sent Kate a photo as soon as I could – a bed selfie. A beddie? Does that sound like a thing? I'll work on that – and she said that, even though I'd just woken up from surgery, the light had come back into my eyes. She said I was glowing. I felt amazing, grateful to be alive. Cancer had done that for me. It had put a filter on my world that I still use to this day – one of gratitude and appreciation that's been with me ever since. I hope it always stays. It's a daily practice for me now to be thankful. So, even when life gets me down, which it does because as we all know life is a little bitch sometimes, I try to remember it's a privilege to be experiencing it. I get to re-emerge in this matrix every day. Every time I wake up, I'm back in the game. It could so easily have been different. I now live each day as a mini lifetime.

I haven't always been able to find this mindset. I was the complete opposite. I learned this lesson the hard way many years ago when something infinitely more heartbreaking to me than cancer sent me hurtling off the rails. I lost myself to fear and grief and I've been trying to find myself ever since. If you're currently struggling through something difficult in your life and it seems like I had it all figured out from the start, it's so important to me that you know that I didn't. I just had the previous experience of knowing that I never wanted to go down that dark path again to teach me how to set off on the right one – for me. There is no 'correct' way to cope with something life-changing; we're all just doing our personal best for wherever we are right now. I used my past to teach me how I wanted to be in my future. I hope this can help you too.

Unbreak My Heart

'She's in love with mourning': Leon from *Gogglebox*. (Hey, I'll take my philosophers wherever I can find them.) I loved hearing Leon say this. It resonated with me so much. It was an episode of *Gogglebox* where they were watching *Downton Abbey* and one of the characters was mourning the loss of someone she loved very deeply. It reminded me of Queen Victoria and how she always wore black after the passing of Prince Albert. She never quite recovered. But maybe she didn't want to? That was me.

Rewind 20 years before my diagnosis to the year 2001. It was the summer of love and I was footloose and fancy-free. Life was good. I was young, I had my whole life ahead of me and I had no real responsibilities. I felt free, like I could go where I wanted and do whatever I wanted. I'd even dropped out of uni. I was supposed to be studying Pharmacology; I told my mum and dad that I was 'taking a year out'. Well, I'm still on that year out as I never went back. *Sings* *All the women who are independent, throw your hands up at me!* Yes, I was having my Destiny's Child moment. *The shoes on my feet? I bought them!*

I had a great job – I was a PA for my Uncle Tony. He had a company that installed satellite dishes for Sky TV. Uncle Tony was so cool! He was married to my mum's older sister, my Auntie Maxine. What a queen. Together they were a dream team. Unstoppable. The life and soul of any party. They were bloody gorgeous, looked after themselves, had stunning clothes, sexy cars and they even had crates of champagne under their stairs. I thought they were so glamorous. It was like the sun always shined on them and, whenever I was around them, I felt that sunshine too. They always seemed so happy and they saw opportunities where others saw problems. They were the kind of people I wanted to be. They lived life to the full and they showed me another way to be.

Day to day I got to look after Uncle Tony and the other directors. I got to see how to run a company, learn from him and get paid for it. Result! I had a company car and I got to work with my sister and my cousin. I loved it. At the weekends, I pursued my passion: DJing. I played at a bar in Preston where I met one of my best friends in the whole world, Fay. Love you, Fay! Fay worked behind the bar with another girl I used to adore who eventually became my girlfriend for a while. Well, kind of – I was obsessed with her, but looking back, she didn't really think much of me. I think she just tolerated me. I don't blame her – I was punching well above my weight. Anyway, I had an amazing life during the week, and it was even better on weekends.

So far so good . . . then everything changed. I remember hearing the news of US R&B superstar Aaliyah passing away and I couldn't believe it. It was so sudden and so tragic. How could this happen? She was in her prime, she had a new album out, she was young, successful, at the top of her game, absolutely beautiful too . . . and so talented. It seemed so cruel. She died in an aeroplane crash flying back from filming a music video. Fay and I were gutted. We loved Aaliyah. I'd play her music in the bar all the time. It didn't feel real. That was in August 2001 and the doom had only just started. Only a few weeks later, the date read the 11th of September 2001: 9/11. Another devastating catastrophic event, but this time involving thousands of people and on a world scale. It was horrific. I remember watching the story as it unfolded with my work colleagues, and then a second plane hit, live on TV. It was absolutely heartbreaking. I was so worried about my cousins who live in New York. I hoped and prayed that they were OK. They were safe thank God, but the trauma of seeing that play out in real time and the effect it had on New Yorkers will stay with us all forever. I felt so bad for everyone. My friends and I were still reeling from Aaliyah; how could two tragic events like that happen so close together? There was no way I was expecting what happened next.

It was October. Halloween in fact. Fay and I had planned to go on a drive up to Pendle Hill to 'see the witches' but something had happened and it got called off. It was the afternoon and I was at work, probably messing about with an Excel spreadsheet or something, when my phone rang. It was my mum. She simply said, 'Can you come home, please, I need to speak to you. Take your time, be careful driving, but come straight home.' OK. I didn't think too much of it. She didn't sound upset so I thought she must be OK, and she didn't sound angry with me – I hadn't done anything naughty recently (or anything she'd have found out about anyway), so I assumed it would be something and nothing. I got into my lovely company car, put on my shades and drove home in the afternoon sun – tunes blaring. It was a beautiful clear day and I even took the scenic route home around the country lanes. I pulled up outside our house and walked in.

To this day, I'm in awe of my mum and so grateful to her for the incredible strength she had. I don't know how she did it. I thought she was asking me to drive carefully because she lost her dad in a fatal car crash when she was just 13. She understandably never came to terms with it. I just don't think she had access to the support that she needed back then. Things were very different. You were just expected to get on with it. I cannot imagine how traumatic and heartbreaking that must have been for her. Her whole world turned upside down in a moment. Her childhood shattered and fractured, never to be the same again. That's just one of many things that my mum has been through. She's an incredible woman.

I arrived back home and walked into the front room ready to hear what she had to say.

'Your Auntie Maxine has died.'

Those words changed my life forever. I have never been the same since. I think a part of me died at that moment too. I always say to Kate that I wish she'd known me before that day. I wish she knew who I used to be – before I got broken, before I transformed beyond repair. I didn't know how to respond, I felt helpless. I just stood there looking at my mum. The worst had already happened. I can't imagine what it took for her to call me. How did she do it? She kept her emotions in so she could keep me safe. I fell forward and collapsed into her. I hugged her with everything I had. I couldn't stop crying. I didn't want to let her go. I wished I could have rewound time and taken those words away. I wished she never had to say them and I'd never heard them. I thought of my Uncle Tony and my cousins, Diane and Kaméo. Was someone looking after them, were they OK? I felt like I couldn't breathe, like I was spinning out of control.

'Where is she, can we go and see her?'

I drove my mum to Southport hospital as calmly and as safely as I could, but inside, my nervous system was in overdrive. I just couldn't believe it. It couldn't be true. That day plays over again and again in my head. I've learned to deal with it much better now, but it's something I know I'll never get over. I think about Auntie Maxine every day. She was like a mother to me, alongside my mum. She was my superstar. She had an amazing life. She made me believe I could achieve anything I wanted. She represented hope to me. I absolutely had her on a pedestal. I wanted to be like her. She made the best of her life. She was a good person. She didn't deserve this. So when she was so cruelly taken, it really sent me off the edge. She'd been ill for the last few days, but it had only seemed like a cold. This wasn't part of the plan. Fate had made a mistake. My guiding light was gone. The day Auntie Maxine died was the day I lost hope. My mum lost her sister, my uncle his beautiful wife and, more devastating than anything, my cousins lost their mum. They didn't even get to say goodbye. I'll never forget walking into the hospital and seeing my little cousin Kaméo's face. She was still in her school uniform, inconsolable. Like my mum when her dad died, she was only 13, and she'd just lost her mum. I felt so selfish in that moment. How could I be so upset when my cousins were going through so much? I think that's when I started to shut down. I didn't allow myself to grieve, I simply buried it. My grief took root and slowly ate away at me from the inside.

Losing Auntie Maxine was too much. Game over. The descent had started. I was falling headlong into the abyss. I went numb. I lost hope. I fell in love with mourning. I didn't have the tools to cope so I just pretended it wasn't happening. I started to self-destruct. I *wanted* to. I didn't want to live my life anymore. I was on autopilot. I made bad choices. I went on *Big Brother*. Can you believe that? To escape my pain, I went into a televised house where they wind you up for fun. AND THEY LET ME! Some people might turn to drink to cope, others to drugs. I turned to Channel 4! I decided to run away. But I couldn't run away from grief: 'It's the price we pay for love.'

Reality (not reality) TV has got much better now and their duty of care has improved a lot. One of the psychiatrists who now works for ITV spoke to me before I went on *I'm a Celeb*. She'd worked on *Big Brother* 3, the series I was in. She said there's no way I would be allowed on the show in that mental state now. Yep, it wasn't my finest moment, but I'm so happy I did it. It taught me so many valuable lessons, and it led me to Kate. I got some sick suitcases out of it too, but, most of all, I took a chance. I'd already fallen into the abyss, my heart was already broken, so I didn't really care what happened to me next. *Big Brother* was one of the rocks I hit on the way down. It actually broke my fall, and I survived. That's when I started the long climb back up.

Why did I do *Big Brother*? People ask me this all the time, and for a long time, I didn't have the answer. I also didn't want to launch into, *Well, my auntie died and it broke my heart. I lost my mind so I decided to go on* Big Brother *instead of being arrested or doing drugs . . . or both.* Was it ego, was it a cry for help? I don't know. I think I just wanted to be as destructive as possible to myself. I think I wanted to do something to help me feel again.

One day, I was aimlessly channel-surfing and flicking between shows on daytime TV. I saw an advert on Channel 4. It was a big spider crawling across a web – it made me want to vom. I hate spiders, but it got my attention. They were looking for people to audition for the third series of *Big Brother*. I'd never watched the show. It wasn't my thing and I couldn't think of anything worse than being on a show like that. For one, they had mirrors everywhere, and for two, I knew they'd see you naked in the shower. No thanks! Deep down, I must have wanted to do it though. Something made me grab a pen and write down the address – no pausing TV in those days; I had to be quick. I guess that was my first big mistake: if you're going to audition for reality TV, at least watch the show. I think the next big mistake was telling the producers I'd never seen it. I think I was the only person that year who'd never seen the show and never auditioned before. I was easy prey.

I went into Southport town centre the next day and straight into Dixons (do you remember Dixons? LOL). I found a video camera that was on sale and bought it because it came with a free tape. I couldn't even afford it – I got it on hire purchase (in those days I still passed credit checks). I took it home, charged it up and did my audition video in one take. If you've ever seen it you can bloody tell. I've still not watched it back properly, but I remember it very well. In fact, there was a bit on the opening night of our series, just before I entered the *Big Brother* house, where they played it on big screens to the crowds and live across the UK to the nation. I remember thinking, *Erm . . . Can you not?*

So back to my bedroom: I was waiting for my new camera to charge and thought about what I could do on my audition tape. *I know*, I thought. I found a Lil' Kim instrumental that I loved – a remix of her song 'Crush On You' – and I wrote a rap to it. Yes, it was just as horrific as it sounds. The video had to be at least 60 seconds long and you had to explain why you should be on *Big Brother*. I did my crap rap and it lasted about 50 seconds. *That'll do*, I thought. I sent it off in the post and didn't think anything of it. And from that point on, I didn't choose to be on *Big Brother*; Big Brother chose me. 'They saw me coming,' as my mum would say.

My audition tape was as tragic as my time on the show – a shit show from start to finish. But everything happens for a reason. Nothing you go through is ever wasted. It all counts. It's only if you don't learn your lesson that history keeps repeating itself. Like a cosmic boomerang, it will find you again and again. There's no escape.

Auntie Maxine was only 42 when she was cruelly taken away from us. I was 42 when I was diagnosed with cancer. I'd already made the mistake of burying my feelings as a 22-year-old. I was young, naive and didn't know how to cope. I didn't ask for help. I should have done. So, on the day of my diagnosis, when I found myself on the edge of another precipice, another point of no return, this time faced with my own mortality, my own brush with death, I knew it was a chance to make different choices. In an instant, my world was crashing down around me. How would I respond this time? Which path would I choose? In a way, it was liberating. I knew it was a chance to do things differently – to rebuild and rise up, not a time to sink back, hide and retreat, back into the comfort of misery. I knew I couldn't control what cancer would do to me, but I could control how I responded to it.

I didn't want to focus on loss; I wanted to focus on life. This time I would allow myself to feel and to grieve. This time I wasn't going to fall in. Not today, Satan. This time I was ready. This time we fly!

NOTE TO SELF:
IT'S NOT WHAT HAPPENS IN LIFE, BUT HOW YOU RESPOND THAT MATTERS.

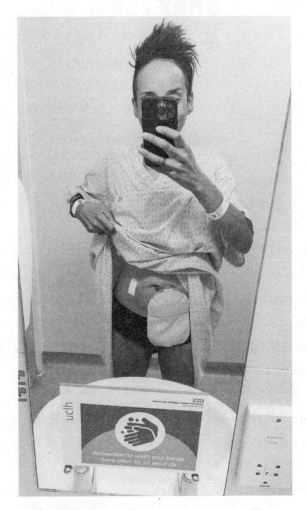

This is Me
Keala Settle

CHAPTER 3

'I am who I'm meant to be.'

This is Me

The ward is my oyster – which lands shall we conquer next? I was starting to see the hospital as my own little gym. This one was amazing and came with its own enhanced recovery workout plan. To be fair, so far in my hospital gym I'd been pretty lazy. My mind had had a good workout, but, apart from that, I'd only sat in a chair. I hadn't even made it past the end of my bed. So, I decided it was time to venture out to the bottom of the bay and see what other activities the hospital had to offer. I was on day three and would like to complete my toilet badge please!

My catheter had been taken out overnight, but I was still hooked up to all sorts of contraptions. I'd already worked out that I could clip some of the tubes onto my nightie and get mobile, but I was a bit worried about the vitamin and drug bags. How would I move with those? They were a pain in the arse when I got in the chair. They're on top of this tall metal pole stand thing, so it kind of meant I had to stay near the bed and I didn't want to stay near the bed – I wanted a ticket to the toilet. What to do?

I asked one of the nurses for advice when she came over. I was hoping she'd say it was OK to go to the toilet. She did, I was allowed – *woohoo!* She swapped my stand for one with wheels so I could make my way over to the other side of the ward and off for a wee. I'd never been so excited about spending a penny. I'd have to go with a chaperone just in case I passed out, but, yep, no worries, coach, get me off the bench and put me in the game. I drank as much water as I could so I'd need to go to the toilet as soon as possible. I couldn't wait to get on that throne. Oh, I knew I was going to love sitting down on that toilet. What a treat. As I chugged another glass of water, I remembered my stoma. *Ooh, what if I take my phone to the toilet?* I could take a photo standing up and have a good look. I could take loads of pictures in there. Imagine if they have a mirror – I could do a selfie. Oh my gosh, THIS WAS THE BEST DAY EVER! The thought of seeing my stoma nearly made me do a wee on the spot. I was like a dog that hadn't seen its owners for a week. My tail was wagging and I was ready to pee.

So there I was: beige, non-slip hospital socks on, bloodied hospital nightie with drainage bag attached, a brand-new metal stand with wheels to help steady me, two carry-on bags (one for vitamins, one for morphine) and a chaperone nurse to complete the look. We were ready. Off we set. I looked like Gandalf, dragging my druggy wizard's staff on our great odyssey to the toilet, with my Frodo nurse by my side in case I fainted.

And we were in. *Dans les toilettes*. ENGAGED. The nurse told me to take my time and to just pull the red emergency cord when I was ready to come out and someone would come and get me. *I'm allowed to pull the emergency cord? That's exciting.* I thanked her for her company on our journey and bid her farewell. I don't know if it was the excitement of the occasion or the amount of water I'd drunk, but I really needed a wee by this point. I stopped and squatted. So far so good. I didn't really notice my stoma bag at that point. It was under my nightie and I couldn't really feel it. I just went to the toilet as normal. Or my new normal. (Only number ones for the foreseeable future; backstage is closed for now, kids.)

I didn't know in that moment just how much toilets would come to feature in my life. Back then, it was just a place to wee. Soon, though, I would know the location of pretty much every public toilet in North London and the surrounding area. It's also usually the first question I ask someone when I enter a new building: *Hello, nice to meet you. Do you have a toilet? Do you mind if I use it?* Stomas are amazing little creatures, but they also come with their challenges. They're not an exact science; each one is different, and every ostomate (someone with a stoma – a stoma is also known as an 'ostomy') has one for a different reason too. Sometimes they're temporary, sometimes they're permanent, sometimes you have more than one, and sometimes they're extremely naughty. That's the type I got – the naughty type. She's a little rascal, but she's my little rascal. Do you know what? I feel very rude not saying her name. It feels weird talking about her and calling her a 'stoma', and as I sit here writing this, I feel like she's a bit pissed with me too. All in good time, Audrey – I'll introduce you properly in a minute.

I finished having my lovely sit-down wee, got myself back up and set about shuffling over to the sink to wash my hands, Gandalf staff in tow. I washed my hands (for 20 seconds with soap and water, coz Covid) and moved to the centre of the sink to look in the mirror. I felt so happy. I was standing up, feeling good and ready to meet my stoma. I lifted up my nightie and peered down. There it was – hanging on the gallery wall of my tummy. *Stoma in Grey*, a work of art. One of the lovely nurses had changed my stoma bag earlier in the day and I was now sporting a svelte, dove-grey bag. Soft and neat and tidy, exactly how Elaine said it would be. She'd also put it in a nice place for me. A few days prior to surgery, Elaine had drawn a black circle with a Sharpie on my torso to signify where my stoma should go if I needed one. Can you imagine the pressure of that? What if you got it wrong? She'd covered up her NHS-approved graffiti tag with a waterproof dressing, but I remember being concerned about it rubbing off during the couple of showers I'd had in the meantime. It didn't, and she nailed that positioning. Looking at it now, my stoma seems to sit just where it needs to be.

OK, overhead shot done, time to go full frontal! I lifted my head and looked at my new body in the mirror. Wow. How fabulous. Again, I didn't know if it was the genius of Elaine, the absurdity of the situation, my brain being in survival mode, or the drugs, but I loved what I saw in the mirror. It just felt right. Though my body might have been a scorched battlefield with smoking embers, a jagged patchwork of holes, scars, bruising and bloating – my own pot belly of pain – it was mine. My parts might have been rearranged, but I was still here, in a different form, with a new space. A place for me to rebuild, reimagine and make even more beautiful. It was my very own kintsugi.

Kintsugi: the Japanese art of repairing broken pottery with gold. It teaches us that if we embrace and value our flaws, mend them with love, then we become stronger and even more beautiful and unique for having been broken.

What a powerful notion. If I could have painted all of my flaws, my wounds and scars in gold, I would have.

My body looked amazing. I've always had a troubled relationship with my body. I'm ashamed to say I'd spent most of my life not really caring about it, covering it up, avoiding looking at it, overeating, sometimes being embarrassed by it. I never felt 'normal'. I didn't appreciate my body. It was always too big, too small, too dark, too light. My skin was a mess too: I had acne, I had scars. I felt ugly. I always wanted to hide away. I gladly wore black. I faded into the background. I wasn't the 'star of the stage' in the story of my life; I was the stagehand. But that day, I fell in love with it. I was so proud. Here was this body, wrestling its way back from the brink, keeping me alive, fighting to see another day and, on top of that, functioning beautifully despite all the trauma it had recently been through. I felt an overwhelming sense of gratitude and appreciation for it. The cancer filter was working its magic again. It felt like, for the first time in my life, I was able to see 'me'. I could have stayed in that toilet for hours looking at myself. It was like I was meeting myself for the first time. I wasn't as hideous as I'd imagined. It felt good not to feel immediate shame when looking at my reflection.

I wasn't broken – I was new, I was mended, I was saved. And I was stronger for it.

Thinking back, we never had mirrors in our house when I was growing up. We just had a small cracked one in the bathroom so my dad could shave. I never used to look in it – I didn't like what I'd see. I also didn't really start seeing my body full length until I went clothes shopping with my friends. It was a shock. Clothes shopping coincided with hormones, with growth spurts and uninvited lumps and bumps. I was transforming, but I didn't feel like a butterfly, I felt like a toad. I didn't look like my friends. They all looked like the girls in the magazines. They were perfect and pretty. I was odd. I looked like Stig of the Dump. I ate my feelings and got really big for my build. I think I was trying to protect myself, to put on some 'padding', to hide myself away. My tactic for dealing with this was to avoid mirrors at all costs. I don't have to look at my face, I thought. I can just peer out of it. If I don't see it, I don't have to worry about it. Magic!

I still don't look in mirrors in shops. I avoid my reflection as much as I can. I'm still learning to reprogram how I see myself. That's why I love my stoma so much – it changed my perception of my body in an instant. All of a sudden, I had a body to be proud of. I could see past the way it looked and fell in love with who it allowed me to be. What it allowed me to do. A bloody beautiful big meat wagon for me to drive! LOL. No more shame.

How had I not realised before how amazing my body was? I'm so lucky to have a body that works. And it's banging. I'm bionic – I've got moving parts. It's a beauty. I grabbed my phone, took a photo and put it in my 'favourites' folder straight away. I couldn't wait to show Kate. Imagine seeing that sliding into your DMs!

Introducing Audrey

OK, Auds – you're on.

It wouldn't be until later that day that my stoma would get her name. Once I'd finished my toilet photo shoot, I pulled the red cord and was escorted back to my cubicle. I popped back into bed to wait for 'the pain team'. How wicked is that name? It amazes me how hospitals work. I don't know how they do it. It's the most brilliant, complicated, yet graceful ballet of different teams and roles all complementing each other in symbiosis throughout the day. The hospital lives and breathes, ebbs and flows, and everyone plays their part perfectly. The pain team are kind of the drug squad. They were there to slowly wean me off the smack (morphine bags) and make sure my enhanced recovery programme was staying on course. That day also marked my first official visit from the stoma nurses.

Up until then, the ward nurses (apologies if that's the wrong term) had been brilliant at changing my stoma bag and looking after it. Now it was time for me to learn how to do it and how to care for it. I imagined it would be like changing a baby's nappy. I've done that before (I've got five younger siblings) – it'll be fine. Looking back, I'd forgotten that babies aren't attached to your torso when you change them and you don't have to cut their nappies to the size of their ever-changing bums. I also hadn't bargained for Audrey, the naughtiest newborn you could ever hope to meet. The stoma nurses were so lovely, kind and smiley, and they came bearing gifts – lots of pamphlets and booklets for me to read and, to my delight, a washbag full of stoma kit. *I get stoma merch? I love merch!* The gorgeous grey washbag, I was told, was to carry all my changing supplies and grey stoma bags. I squealed because it all matched. I was going to look SO swanky in that bathroom. Matching luggage, baby.

The nurses explained that they were going to show me what to do and, from the next day, I'd have to do it myself. *Excuse me? Come again? Me, myself and I? Me? On my ACTUAL own?* And, I had to do it with the nurses watching . . . just to check. I started to get nervous. I hadn't really thought about this property. I just assumed the NHS fairies would do it while I was in hospital, and then I'd go home and palm it off on Kate. She loves crafty stuff. She'd be buzzing. I fixed the nurses with a forced, wide-eyed grin and swiped my phone from the bedside table: 'Do you mind if I FaceTime Kate while you show me what to do?'

The stoma nurses were so patient; they had no idea who Kate was, and, to be fair, my request was a bit niche. I'm not sure many people ask to film a stoma bag change and FaceTime their girlfriend while it's happening.

So there we were, me on the infamous high-backed chair – nightie up, pants down, stoma out – with Kate propped up on the window ledge, watching remotely. The nurses made it all look so easy. They were the pit crew of stoma changing. Kate, the crafty little swot, seemed to follow along with ease. I, on the other hand, was overwhelmed. This is the only time I've wanted to hand the stoma back.

'I . . . I can't look after it. I'll accidentally kill it! If my stoma dies, do I die too?'

Oh, those sweet, sweet stoma nurses. The patience of SAINTS! They managed to calm me down and return me to bed, newly changed, with the reassurance that it'd all be fine in the morning. Before they left, one of them asked me if I'd thought of a name for my stoma yet. Some people name them to help with the mental recovery process, especially if, like me, you've not known for long that you're going to have one. It can help you to sort of 'bond' with it.

Me: 'Yes, she's got a name!'

Stoma nurse: 'Ooh what have you picked?'

Me: 'Audrey.'

Stoma nurse: 'Oh, that's a lovely name! Like Audrey Hepburn?'

Me: 'No, have you seen *Little Shop of Horrors?*'

At this point, I think if there'd been a panic button nearby, the nurse would have pressed it. I noticed a flicker of concern on her face and a subtle glance to her colleague. I think the mention of the word 'horror' on top of all the recent filming malarkey made them worry I might not be as mentally well-adjusted as they first thought.

Me: 'She's named after the plant in that. My girlfriend Kate played Audrey in the stage musical once, and the stoma looks like the cute little plant in the movie.'

They each let out a relieved breath and nodded to each other, apparently placated by my explanation.

Stoma nurse: 'Oh, well, good. Lovely! OK, well here's your bag. And some things to read. The nurse will be here later to help you change your bag, and tomorrow . . . it's your go!'

I nodded, totally blagging that I was OK with all of this, and waved them off with a big smile.

I looked in the kit bag. It was full of things I didn't recognise and instruments I'd never seen before. WTF was it all? I turned a stoma bag over in my hand; I'd never really got a good look at one properly before. The back of the bag, the bit that Audrey should fit in, looked like an archery target with concentric circles on it. What were all these rings for? What do the numbers mean? Would I have to measure Audrey to see what size circle she is? Thank God I was getting help that evening. I'd just had my theory test . . . tomorrow, it would be my practical exam.

Every Day's a School Day

I woke up nervous. It's stoma school day. Like leg day at the gym, you don't want to do it, but it's necessary. Like my Uncle Tony used to say, 'Never skip leg day,' and he had sensational legs.

The stoma nurses would be here soon to assess my skills. I was prepared for the odd major fault and a few minors, but fingers crossed I'd ace the rest and pass my stoma bag driving test. Until then, I busied myself with my new routine: a trip down exercise alley (a long corridor I'd discovered just around the corner from my ward with 'way to go!' victory bunting and posters of gentle exercises on the wall designed to rehabilitate me and any other fellow gym bunny patients who were up for the challenge), a nip to the toilet for a little peek and a wave at Audrey and then on to a good session looking out of the window at the London skyline and the streets below. Oh, how I loved it! I'd spend hours at that window, like a cat on a sill watching the world go by. Especially the sky – nature's moving masterpiece, all contained within my hospital window frame.

Looking down, I was treated to the merry dance of people and cars in the streets below. It was fascinating watching their non-stop ebb and flow. All on their own separate journeys, cosmically brought together and now moving as one – the physical heartbeat of the city. I'd wonder where they were going, what they might be doing, what they might be thinking. I hoped they were happy. I hoped they were having a good day. I wondered if they knew we were up here watching them go by. There were so many people behind these windows who would have swapped places with them in a heartbeat. Some of the people up here with me might never get to walk those streets again. I made a mental note. I hoped that if I was lucky enough to get back down there, I'd make the most of it. I'd always remember the people on this side of the glass. I'd appreciate the gift of feeling those streets beneath my feet. If I ever got overwhelmed, if I ever started to forget how lucky I was, all I'd need to do is look up.

'Zoom in and obsess, zoom out and observe.'
– Rick Rubin

I heard some footsteps behind me and turned to see two young stoma nurses with big, hopeful smiles. My instructors were here! They popped themselves into my driving bay, closed the curtain, and it was time to begin my test.

I've never been good at arts and crafts. The moment I realised that putting a new stoma bag on involved scissors, it was game over. *Deborah Meaden voice* *I'm out*, I thought, *I'm not investing*. My creative abilities stretch as far as colouring in. Anything more complicated than that ends in disaster. I'm still scarred from home economic classes at high school, or 'home EC' as we used to call it. I was actually looking forward to them before I realised what they entailed. Part of getting ready for home EC was buying a basket – a real-life basket, formed from wicker, and my mum would have to allow it because the school said so. It was the sort of thing I'd only ever heard about in fairy tales or seen in movies. The basket was to carry our ingredients into school. I was so excited – I felt like a real-life lady. I used to skip cheerily out of my council estate on home EC days feeling real posh. I'd also heard that home EC involved learning how to use a sewing machine. *Oh, this class is immense*, I thought. *I'll be able to cook and make my own clothes out of curtains in no time. I'll be unstoppable.* This was going to be a doddle. I used to help my nana with her baking so I was confident with that. Both my nana and Auntie Val were also whizzes on a sewing machine, and I absolutely loved them. Auntie Val was always buzzing away making clothes. My cousin Christine was a Morris dancer in a championship-winning troupe and Auntie Val would help to make all the costumes. I felt so sorry for my classmates – I was going to pass this class with flying colours. I already had the cheat codes; it was in my blood.

Well, speaking of blood . . . I not only managed to accidentally sew my finger into a seam during one of the classes, but I also failed my 'sewing machine driving test'. Yep, they actually called it that! I failed so many times that, in the end, they had to just pretend I'd passed so I could sit inside the classroom and not on the outside. I was the only one who failed IN THE WHOLE SCHOOL. Or at least that's what the teacher told me. The cooking side of things wasn't much better either. We ended up making all sorts: bread, pineapple upside-down cake, pizza. I had quite the repertoire (on paper), and I'd skip back home from school, carrying my fresh hot bakes in my basket, eager to show my mum my handiwork. The moment I got home, she would lovingly take whatever I'd made out of my basket and put it straight in the bin. I'm not joking. She didn't even pretend to give it a go. I think I'd mixed up salt and sugar in one of the recipes once. She tried it, never again. From then on, she didn't want to take her chances. Even the bloody pizza! I told her that one was safe because my teacher ended up making my dough for me (that's how terrible I was), all I'd done was the topping, and she still wouldn't eat it. Bloomin' cheeky if you ask me, LOL.

Yeah, so home EC was never my forte. I didn't bake again for years. I swerved flour, yeast and baking powder like the plague. It wasn't until I was asked to take part in *The Great British Bake Off* for Stand Up To Cancer in 2022 that I even considered putting a pinny back on again. How could I refuse? It was a no-brainer. That show is incredible – every single person who takes part has a large donation made to Cancer Research on their behalf. No exceptions, that's the deal. The show donates, you bake. Cancer Research gets thousands of pounds and you get new skills . . . and friends. Sign me up! I not only got to share a tent with the powerhouse that is Prue Leith and Paul 'Dreamy Blue Eyes' Hollywood, but I also got to bake alongside three legends: the very lovely and extremely funny Lucy Beaumont (I think Lucy might be the funniest person alive – my stomach hurt so much from laughing at her), the charming, suave and delightful David Morrissey, and one of the finest specimens of human being I've ever witnessed, the man of my Olympic dreams, Tom Daley. All brought together by the fabulous Matt Lucas and Noel Fielding. Being in that tent was an absolute joy from start to finish. It was just what I needed. We filmed *Bake Off* a few weeks after I'd finished chemotherapy and it was something good for me to look forward to, something to keep me going. It made my time on the show even more meaningful. I felt very lucky to have been offered chemo, but, as we'll talk more about in a while, by the end of the six-month course, it was getting really tough; in fact it was brutal. My body was clapped out, knackered, broken and bloated. I couldn't maintain my temperature properly and I'd constantly overheat. (The lovely production team on *Bake Off* arranged for me to have an ice machine because of this.) The show gave me purpose. It helped me focus. I got to learn something new. I became someone new. I raised the upper limits of my personal best. I wanted to make the most of my second chance at life. This was an opportunity to reimagine myself and rewrite the script.

That's how powerful belief is. Maybe I wasn't as shit as I'd imagined after all. Maybe I just had one rubbish bake at school and then that turned into a lifetime of bad bakes. Bad thoughts. Maybe I was subconsciously proving myself right. Chemo might have been breaking me down, but it was changing my perspective too – not only removing any lingering cancer cells from my body, but taking their bad energy and negativity with them, symbolically and physically removing all the junk I'd accumulated over the years. I was becoming a blank canvas of sorts. It was giving me a good clear out, giving me a free refit. I was still the same building, but I had a chance to redecorate. A chance to reimagine the space. A chance to rebuild and become a better person. The person I needed to see when I was younger.

This was my chrysalis. I was transforming from a caterpillar to a butterfly. There's a beautiful poem by Rupi Kaur ('representation' in *the sun and her flowers*) which talks about the importance of representation and how, if a butterfly was only surrounded by moths, it would think there was something wrong with it, when really they're both just as beautiful as each other.

I think I'm more of a moth than a butterfly, to be fair – a moth that loves wearing black, LOL. That's just how I identify. But it's important for me to become the best bloody moth I can be. Once I got Audrey, it broke my heart to realise how many ostomates didn't feel understood or included by society. I couldn't understand it. A lot of them feel shame. That hurt me so much on their behalf. Every single ostomate is an inspiration to me. They don't just hand these things out like sweets, you know – you've got to earn them. You've got to have been through a really tough time to get one. That operation hurts like hell – I've never felt pain like it – and then it's a long road to recovery. Sometimes it's also a lonely experience, as wonderful and supportive as others can be. So every time I see an ostomate, I know they're made of tough stuff. I know they've had to dig deep – both physically and mentally. I also totally understand if they don't like their stoma or they don't want to talk about it or share it. I'm not surprised. It can be a traumatic experience. Some people may go from feeling like a 'normal' well-adjusted member of the public to someone who's not represented or accommodated by society. They might feel like they've become an outsider. That's how I've spent most of my life feeling. For me, though, cancer and chemo gave me common ground. It helped people to see me. I never used to really see women who looked like me on TV when I was younger, and if I did, people used to think they were odd. Sometimes people didn't see those women at all. In the same way, it felt like most people couldn't see me before all of this and, to be fair, I quite liked it. I liked being invisible. It was what I was used to. But from time to time I didn't understand it. Society doesn't always value all of its parts, which is a shame, and that needs to change. More gatekeepers need to move the gateposts and welcome more people through. Look at all of the beauty and variety in nature. We *are* nature. We're supposed to be unique. It's beautiful. It makes life richer.

The more colours we allow to shine through, the better the rainbow.

So existing in a world that didn't seem to value or recognise bodies like mine made it that much easier to accept my stoma. It wasn't taking anything away from me, it was adding to me. It was enriching me. Both physically and mentally, it was also changing me. This was no time to hide. I finally had something to say that I believed would be heard. Cancer and chemo were my Trojan Horse. They opened up the gates, the keepers allowed me in and I could celebrate ostomates for all to see. I went from being invisible to being normal. It was cool being in the majority for a change. I could be that person I needed to see when I was younger. We're not odd, or weird, or strange, or a burden . . . we're absolute warriors! It was also time to refocus. I wasn't at all worried about what I now couldn't do. All I could see was the possibility. When you start to appreciate what you already have, you'll realise you have blessings in abundance. I nearly lost it all. I not only got my life back, I got my body back.

So to my fellow stoma crew and those dealing with cancer: Your body may have changed, but so have you – from your innermost core to the crown at the top of your head. You are richer for this experience. You now have added value. You've just completed your own marathon. So don't just get to the gates of your community and stop. Stride in like the hero you are and tell your story. Be proud of what you've achieved. Don't believe the cancer, chemo and stoma propaganda. That's old news. Deep down, we're all the same – we are all made of stars, just as wonderful, beautiful, unique, odd and imperfectly perfect as anyone else. It's what makes us human.

Maybe the transformation isn't about butterflies or moths. Maybe we've been caterpillars all this time, plodding along.

Maybe life has just handed us a pair of wings. Don't be afraid to fly.

The body is merely a wrapper to clothe the soul. It's time for all of us to shine.

Oh gosh, I'm so sorry, I got a little sidetracked there! I get quite passionate about ostomates and cancer. OK, back to the task at hand, and to the burning question: Would I fail my stoma bag driving test?

I don't want to sound hysterical, but if you can change a stoma bag, you should automatically be inducted into Mensa. It felt like I'd been asked to build a fully functional spaceship from scratch with no instructions, out of Lego. It seemed impossible. Magic spray, scissors, dry wipes, wet wipes, more dry wipes, measuring stuff, cutting circles, doggie bags for the rubbish. What did it all mean?! I'll be honest, the stoma nurses helped me a lot. My first attempt to change Audrey reminded me of the times when my mum would be away and my dad would try to get us ready for school. Yes, technically we were 'dressed', but we left the house looking like we'd already done a full day at school, been swimming and got ourselves dressed again. We were dishevelled, like crumpled bags of crisps, before we'd even started. In my case, my child Audrey would have been better doing it herself.

As I'd learn in the coming weeks, Audrey was a two-person job, not to be tackled alone. Luckily, on my first go, I had my stoma nurse *sensei* to guide me through the process. They did their best to impart their wisdom and knowledge to me and, to be fair, after we'd finished, Audrey was technically secured behind the bag. I probably did a good 70 per cent of the work on my own. When I finished, the bag was stuck to my body, it was defying gravity and it was neatly tucked into my knickers. Buzzing! Job's a good 'un! Thank you, *sensei*. I am ready.

I'd had another great day of small steps and small wins and they were starting to stack up. I was getting more confident, stronger and learning how to navigate the world with my new body. I was learning to walk with the physio team, doing my daily workout in exercise alley and keeping myself moving – my daily little rebellion against cancer. I felt good. I felt empowered. Little wins gave me big hope. I went to bed that night, having completed my first solo bag change, feeling super proud. I lay in my hospital bed smiling to myself, one hand placed gently near Audrey, my new hot water bottle (she's surprisingly warm).

My newly named little friend would sleep like a baby tonight. She would be kind to me. Tomorrow she'd wreak havoc and have me crying by the end of the day. Just like the plant in *Little Shop of Horrors*, she'd realised her power, and she was ready to take over my world.

NOTE TO SELF:
THERE IS BEAUTY IN IMPERFECTION.

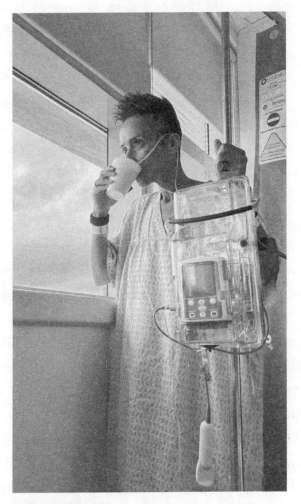

Rain on Me
Lady Gaga & Ariana Grande

CHAPTER 4

'I'd rather be dry, but at least I'm alive.'

Rain on Me

It was a funny feeling. A warm, oozing sensation slowly creeping across my body. It was quite nice actually – a comforting embrace, like a blanket swaddling my soul, then . . . BAM! My eyes opened and I realised sewage was pouring out of the hole on the front of my body. It was as though there was a hosepipe in my bed, but it was me – I WAS the hosepipe. All the lovely, cosy warmth was gone in an instant and I was cold and wet and past the point of no return. The bed was wrecked. *Shit.* Literally. To be fair to Audrey, and sorry if this is TMI, she doesn't actually do 'proper' poos. Because she's an ileostomy, my digestive system now ends at my small intestine, which means any waste that comes out of me is more like what you'd expect from a baby – still not exactly pleasant, but a bit more . . . mild? LOL. Apparently all the hardcore adult stuff is made in the large intestine and I don't have access to that section for a while until it heals from my surgery. This means that what the stoma nurses politely call the 'output' (poo) can often be quite watery, and that's exactly what I'd just woken up in – a tsunami of Audrey's mess. It was like a burst water main. Liquids and sticky seals on stoma bags don't always mix and the bag that I'd been so proud of changing earlier that day hadn't stood a chance against Audrey's tidal wave.

It was around midnight when I woke up in a panic, wondering who was hosepiping me and then the realisation that I'd wet the bed set in. I felt so embarrassed. I took full responsibility; it was my fault. I hadn't put the bag on properly. Plus, it wasn't normal 'wet the bed' wee. It was Audrey poo-wee, all over the crisp white sheets that had been changed earlier that day. I was absolutely mortified. I wanted to cry.

Telling this story back, it seems understandable that my first attempt at a stoma bag change hadn't held up, but at the time, it felt like a disaster. It took me down a few pegs. Who did I think I was? I wasn't getting better. I was still ill. It felt like cancer was winning and I was dreaming. It felt physically demeaning and mentally devastating. The act of losing my bag chipped away at my hope. It allowed the doubt to creep in and the devil to climb onto my shoulder once again: 'Oh you thought you were doing well? You thought you were getting out of here? You thought you were in control? You can't even change a stoma bag. You've pissed yourself. You're an idiot, how pathetic.'

How could I go home now? How could I tell Kate that I can't even go to the toilet properly? I can't control my bowels. I'm not strong, my body is weak. I'm like a baby. What will my

mum and dad think? They raised me better than this. I've let
them down.

I didn't know what to do. I lay there in the cold, wet mess for
a good ten minutes just staring at the ceiling, wondering how I
could get out of it. I couldn't. I couldn't escape – I had to ask for
help.

> 'Ask every failure, what is this here to teach me?
> As soon as you get the lesson, you get to move on.'
> – Oprah Winfrey

Well said, Oprah. That night was a big lesson for me. It taught me
to accept help and that it's OK to lean on people. That there's
strength in being honest – it's brave to be vulnerable; it's not a
weakness. There have been so many times in my life when I wish
I'd asked for help and let people in. I'm still learning this lesson.

Eventually, I plucked up the courage to call the nurse.
I'll never forget it. She came into my bay, the light at the
side of my bed illuminating her face as she smiled, 'Are you
OK?'

I looked at her for a moment and thought, *Can't you see? I'm
covered in Audrey's sewage and I've wrecked the bed. There's mess
everywhere! It's a crime scene. You're literally going to have to
cordon me off and burn the bed.* Then it dawned on me. The
nurse could only see what was presented in front of her – a hospital patient tucked up safely in bed. She had no idea about the
carnage under the covers.

'I'm so sorry, I've had an accident,' I whispered, and as I pulled back the covers to show her, I burst out crying. All of the emotion flooded out of me. The dam had burst, and despite my attempt to hold back the tide, I cried like a baby. I was defeated; I felt so much shame.

'It's all right,' she said, giving me a tissue. 'Things like this happen. You'll have leaks. It happens to everyone. It's OK. I'll be back in a minute,' and that was it. Simple, calm and kind. Perception had gotten the better of me. Sometimes the monsters we fear are much worse in our heads. I was reacting to how I was feeling. It wasn't the full picture, it wasn't reality – it was 'my reality'. I will never forget this moment and the way she said those words. She didn't shout. She didn't laugh at me. She simply understood. I'd admitted defeat – I'd CRIED! – and the world hadn't ended. It might sound so strange, but this was a huge revelation to me – that it's OK to let things out.

Until this moment, I had spent a lifetime locking my feelings inside. I thought it was strong to keep things in, to not show weakness. *Don't cry.* Even as a kid, I didn't ever cry when I hurt myself. I've been thinking about this a lot recently. As I've been writing this book I've uncovered a lot of things that I'd pushed to the back of my mind – some of the things I'd forgotten are scary. How do you not remember a brick to the skull?

I was about six or seven. My parents were arguing with one of our 'neighbours' who lived across the road. Mum and Dad were in our garden and she was on the other side, standing on a small brick wall at the front of her house.

I came out of the house to see their tormentor. She was a slight woman and she was pretty. Well, she had bleached blonde hair with black roots and wore electric blue mascara, so to me, in the eighties, she was practically a supermodel. She was Barbie. Council Estate Barbie. And Barbie was rampaging out of her box. It got bad. My dad was holding back my mum – good luck with that, Dad! As strong as he was at that time, the way Mum was moving, that would have taken a lot of force. I'm not sure what happened next, but things seemed to escalate very quickly. The supermodel jumped down from her wall and picked up a broken brick from her garden. I think it might have been a bit of the wall she was standing on that had fallen away. I thought she was going to go back inside her house and chuck the jagged missile away, but no, she ran into the middle of the road and threw the brick towards my mum. I was horrified. *No, not my mum!* Maybe the brick heard me. It hit me instead, with full force at the front of my head. The pain was immediate; it felt like she'd cracked my skull wide open. The most intense burning sensation shot right around the plates of my head and then careered down into my body. It was like I'd been struck by lightning. I immediately put my hands to my head – it was slippery to the touch. I was told not to cry. Don't show weakness. Don't show fear. I held my breath. I held back the tide. The burning stayed within, ricocheting around my body and being locked in forever. I swallowed the key.

I had totally forgotten about this brick incident until I shaved my head when I started chemo. How messed up is that? One of many things that I've 'forgotten', I guess. Kate couldn't believe it when I showed her the scar. It's an indentation about the size of a one pound coin. Maybe that's when I learned not to cry when I hurt myself, however the hurt happened.

I can't actually remember a time when I didn't have worry in my tummy – it was my default setting as a child. I've always felt like that. Maybe that's what cancer was sent here to teach me. Maybe it's a physical manifestation of everything I've been burying and ignoring. My brain might have forgotten it, but what if the body remembers? They say that energy cannot be created or destroyed, it can only be transformed. If that little kid didn't cry . . . where did that energy go? I don't know. But what I *do* know is that once that tumour was removed, it felt like it took years of bad energy with it. I felt free. Like Kate said, the light came back into my eyes.

I've heard that the gut is like a second brain. Maybe my Audrey's here to teach me how to really be brave. To be vulnerable, to let things in and, most importantly, to let things out. Maybe my gut is here to show me what really having guts is all about?

It's the work we do in the dark that leads us to the light.

I went to sleep that night with my bag changed and personally changed for the better. There'd be many more mistakes and leaks in my future: some of them in the Radio 1 studio, some of them just before I was about to go on daytime TV. But I was OK with that. Shit happens – literally. Life goes on, and one thing I knew for sure is that this little tormentor in my pants was keeping me alive.

NOTE TO SELF:
THERE IS STRENGTH IN VULNERABILITY.

Make it Happen (Live at MTV Unplugged)
Mariah Carey

CHAPTER 5

'If you believe in yourself enough

and know what you want . . .'

Make it Happen

Kate and I are absolutely buzzing. We're singing our hearts out with an impromptu Vengaboys-inspired freestyle: 'The stoma nurse is coming and everybody's jumping,' to the tune of the Vengaboys' classic, 'We Like to Party'.

Yes, we are getting ready for the arrival of Elaine the stoma nurse. She rang to say she's on her way. She's actually coming to our house. OMG! What will she be like outside of the hospital? We've never seen her in real life. Will it be like seeing your teacher outside of school and you freak out? Will we accidentally call her 'Mum'? Will we finally get to see the bottom of her face or will she still have to wear a mask? What biscuits should we get in for her? Have we got coffee and sugar in?

Kate is so excited for our VIP's arrival that she's actually tidying up and putting out her posh candles. Can you believe it? Kate is *tidying up*. Wow, what a day! Kate usually gets a pass with her mess because she's the 'creative' one. Since we've lived in this tiny flat, Kate has infiltrated every surface possible. She's slowly taking over. She's crept her way into every nook and cranny she can find – the ultimate space invader. Books, clothes, shoes, toiletries . . . she's like TK Maxx. Shelves and surfaces are rammed with stuff she doesn't use but claims she *needs*. Cupboards are brimming and bursting at the seams, exploding with tat when you open them. She is the yin to my yang. I am basic. The bare minimum. Bog standard. I like to keep it simple. Just like the great philosopher (and rapper) Pitbull once said, K.I.S.S.: Keep It Simple, Stupid. Great advice.

Tidying up is usually my job. I bloody love tidying up. I also love washing up, doing laundry, putting the bins out and, most of all, going to the shops. Corner shops and discount stores are my favourite. I could stay in them all day, really taking my time walking around their retail maze from start to finish, seeing what's new, scanning the shelves and finding bargains. I do Kate's head in. I'm that person who will happily walk the full length of IKEA. She just wants to buy her tea lights, cut through round the back and grab a 50p hotdog on the way out. I think my love of shops began with my mum. She used to work at Kwik Save. I thought she was *it*. She was so glamorous and cool in her crisp uniform, big gold hoops and bright red tabard. What a woman. She reminded me of Quentin Tarantino's Jackie Brown (without the cocaine smuggling). She was a master of the checkout, possessing the speed of the swipe and the perfection of the bag pack. She never squashed your eggs or your bread. Her elegant hands would then deftly find the perfect combination of coins and notes out of her till to give you your change – coins first then the notes – the sign of a true pro (the other way around is super annoying). Yes, I'm the daughter of a checkout virtuoso. To this day, I can rack, stack and pack with the best of them. Kate's cupboards are full of tat. Mine are like a mini supermarket, everything facing the front and in perfect rows. I find so much peace in the simple act of putting things in order – over and over. I love the mundane, I love repetitive action. It's so calming to me. I need routine. I've learned this as I've gotten older. It's how I cope with life.

Routine as a child gives us stability. Routine as an adult gives us purpose.

My dad, a builder by trade, taught me that if you lay one brick, and then another, and then another, eventually, you'll have a house. You don't have to worry about how you're going to build the whole house straight away – you just have to focus on one brick. Start small, dream big. That's the magic, that's the secret sauce. Small acts, repeated over time, can move mountains. Even the Grand Canyon started as a trickle of water. Those little drops eventually caused a chasm so big you can see it from space! Whenever I've achieved a big goal, it's always started with something small.

From Paper Bag to Record Bag

So, how do you achieve your dream job of being a Radio 1 DJ? Jump on your BMX and get yourself a paper round of course – you never know where it could lead. I didn't have a plan. I didn't even think for one minute about the bigger picture. I just wanted to earn enough money so I could spend every penny on my first love, my BFF, my forever friend, yep – music. Music has always been there for me and will never let me down. It is my instant portal away from any of my grey days, my magical passport to musical Wonderland. Music is the friend that ignites my soul and makes my heart sing.

As soon as I was old enough to pass as a paper girl, I took my chance, and I was away – 6p a house was my tariff. I quickly learned that the paper rounds were given out on a first come, first served basis, meaning that, if I got up early enough, I could just about fit in three rounds, do about a hundred houses and earn around £6 a week – cash in hand – all by my own pedal power. I WAS RICH! Do you realise how many cassettes and CDs I could get from Woolworths with that? Plus, if I got lucky in the Woolies bargain basket, I would still have some money left over for pick 'n' mix. I was absolutely balling.

That little Sunday job would set me on a path that would change my life. Those quiet, solitary Sunday mornings, paper bag heaving and houses expecting, would all eventually lead to one very special Sunday night. A Sunday night far in the future, far down the undulating river of life, a cascade that would eventually carry me to just the right place at just the right time, washing me aboard the good ship BBC.

'Every action is a vote for the sort of person you wish to become.'
– James Clear, *Atomic Habits*

My mum and dad were my proof that small actions, repeated over time, equals progress. They valued get-up-and-go, forward momentum, making your own way in the world. They taught me that, if you want something, you have to go out and get it yourself – that you have to be willing to do the things that others won't. They showed me that any positive action, no matter how small or simple, always pays off in the end. Keep moving forward in your life, and your time will never be wasted. I saw every job I ever had as an opportunity to learn and get paid for it. In a way, I was getting paid to go to school, at the age of 11! What a way to start my degree at the great university of life. So off I went, stacking my metaphorical bricks, swiping goods across my imaginary checkout and delivering Sunday newspapers to the good people of Southport.

By the age of 16, I'd traded in my paper round for the prestigious role of glass collector at my dad's friend's nightclub. Now you're talking – I'd hit the big time. Not only was it a pay rise, but it was an absolute masterclass on how to give people the time of their lives. I thought it was all so glamorous: late nights, disco lights and people dressed up to the nines, all spending their hard-earned money and living like rock stars, each and every weekend. I fell in love with it all, and then . . . I fell for the man in the corner. Well, his *job*. That's when I knew what I wanted to be. That was the night the DJ changed my life.

Slowly but surely, I swapped my cassette tapes for vinyl. I studied the DJ and watched him effortlessly work the room each and every night. Alan, a cheeky chappy and loveable Scouser, had charisma in abundance; he was our local superstar. He was the ultimate maestro and the perfect gentleman. He took me under his beautiful, bronzed wing and became my mentor. He was so good to me. He'd answer my endless questions, teach me how to use the kit and give me advice as often as he could. How kind is that? I couldn't afford decks and he knew it – they cost thousands – so he let me use his and, thanks to his generosity and support, I could practise and slowly teach myself to mix. Always at the end of the night though, when nobody was watching or listening – which was a blessing in disguise really because I was spectacularly dreadful for a LONG time! It'd take me years to learn how to do it properly. I could only practise at weekends, and this was way before the internet, so no YouTube tutorials for me. I had to try to work it out for myself. I was famous for doing the 'falling down the stairs' mixing technique, which basically means that, because I didn't know what I was doing, the records I was supposed to be 'mixing' were so out of time that it sounded like a herd of elephants falling down the stairs. Ha ha. I didn't care though; I was earning, I was learning, and I was stupidly happy.

To this day, I don't ever worry about being rubbish at something – that's pretty much been the story of my life. I've learned over the years that, for me, hard work beats natural talent. If you don't give up, you can't be stopped, and you'll always get there in the end. Plus, mistakes are all part of the journey – they're cosmic course-correctors to point you in the right direction. I was laughed at and ridiculed so much, whether it was the fact that I was a woman DJing (there weren't many female DJs in those days – especially not in local nightclubs), my shoddy mixing skills or the sight of me buying records in my school uniform. I titillated and amused others regularly and I was mocked and misunderstood much more than I was encouraged . . . but I never let it deter me. Every bit of progress, no matter how small, felt like a victory to me. Spending my days with my first love – my sweet, sweet music – was an absolute triumph. How could I be deterred when I had music on my side? Music lifts me up more than any insult could ever bring me down.

To me, no effort is ever wasted. If you're learning and growing, then you're always making progress. You're playing smart in the game of life. You're becoming the person you need to be so that when the time is right, you're ready to go. They say luck is preparation meeting opportunity, and if you never give in, eventually your time will come.

So, from delivering papers, to collecting glasses, it was off to Leeds – to university – where I found myself stumbling into radio. I'd only gone to fresher's week to get some free tins of beans, but by the end of the day I'd signed up to be part of LSR, Leeds Student Radio, and pitched for my own radio show. Was I delusional? Why did I do this? The cheek of me! I asked if I could present a two-hour mix show where I simply played records but didn't speak. AT ALL. And can you believe it, they said yes. Thank goodness they did, because when I actually came to do the show, I was so terrified the words wouldn't have come out anyway and, despite my best efforts, there were still a lot of elephants falling down the stairs whenever I tried to do a mix.

Fail Fast, Fail Forward

As you can probably tell, I was pretty terrible at being a radio presenter too. I was a joke and a disaster for many years. I've had a carnage of a career. I even sacked *myself* from ASDA FM once (true story, LOL). I've had enough cock-ups to write a whole other book. Even my dad told me I was rubbish (thanks, Dad). But for some reason, and somehow, I just kept going. I kept learning, kept on experimenting, often failing but failing forward – on repeat. I was undeterred. I can't tell you how many times I was told 'no', or that I wasn't good enough, or I'd never make it in a month of Sundays. Sometimes I'd get no response at all. But I took it all on board – I took it all as an opportunity to work on myself, improve and be better. I set high standards for myself and I gave myself low expectations of the world. That way, I was never disappointed. If I couldn't find a way through, I'd sidestep and go the long way around.

If it's not become apparent already in this chapter, then let me say it again. I mess up ALL THE TIME. But that's OK, because I truly feel that when something is meant to be, it will be – by hook or by crook. You can mess up, but you can never really mess it up, whatever it is for you; 'nothing meant for you will pass you by,' as the memes go. Opportunities and lessons will keep presenting themselves and coming back around until you get the memo, you just need to be present enough to heed it. If you try your best, you can't lose. You can only learn lessons or win. That's how I see it anyway. And this faith within me – or this incredulous level of stupidity, however you wish to see it – always pays off in the end.

In the words of *Strictly* judge Craig Revel Horwood, my first brush with the BBC was 'a total disaaaaaster darling'! It was 2001, and the BBC was launching a cool new digital radio station, code-named 'Network X'. Open days were to be held across the UK to find up-and-coming producers, artists and DJs to be part of it. From the moment I read about it, I wanted in. It sounded like a dream: a brand-new radio station, starting from scratch, looking for new voices, faces and ideas. I hoped I could be part of the team. I'd still only done a bit of presenting on student radio at that point and I was ropey AF, but hey, I can learn, I thought. So off I went with Fay, all the way to Birmingham in my little red car. It took us over three hours to get there. The traffic was rammed, but I didn't care – as long as I made it into that room before they finished, I felt I was in with a chance. We ran as fast as we could to the hall where the open day was being held, super excited and eager to see who was there and to hear what they had to say. I practically fell into the room, took one look at all the super cool DJ people from London, heard the banging tunes that one of them was spinning in the corner, and absolutely shit myself. I was terrified. I froze. I was nearly sick on the spot. I felt so intimidated, so foolish, so small. I was out of my depth. *I don't belong in this room.* It was way above my station. Who did I think I was? I didn't even dare to look at anyone, let alone talk to them. Fay and I did a couple of laps around the room. I spoke to literally NO ONE and then walked straight back out to the car. Yep, I was that idiot. To this day, I don't think anyone else knows I was there that afternoon apart from Fay.

'Well, that was a waste of time, mate,' she said as we began the long, sad drive back home. And, after a few moments of silence and despite my feelings of dejection, failure and embarrassment, I started to laugh. I was raging and I so didn't want to laugh at the time, but Fay does that to me. She has this way of always making things feel better. No matter how bad. She'd also be there for me again later that year when Auntie Maxine passed away. I know I don't tell you enough, Fay, but please know you've helped me more in life than you could ever know.

Even though I thought I'd blown my chance and that I'd never be good enough to join Network X, I couldn't stop thinking about it. My heart wouldn't let me – even when I messed things up a little bit more. A year later, by the end of 2002, I'd made a huge tit of myself on *Big Brother*, and Network X had become the glorious national DAB station BBC Radio 1Xtra. The gap had widened. I was an even bigger sad effort loser, and nobody would touch me with a bargepole. 1Xtra was now the exciting new beacon of youth radio, broadcasting across the UK, championing new black music and celebrating black culture. It was even more incredible than I had imagined – I was in love. I truly never thought I'd make it on; I was just so happy it was here and I could admire it from afar. Life for me in Southport carried on – I'd just keep learning, growing and chipping away at myself in the background with the hopes that one day I'd maybe be considered. And if it didn't happen, then I was OK with that too. At least I'd tried. It's the not trying that would have made me feel like a real failure. I believe that if you put out positive energy, work hard and have good intentions, anything can happen. And eventually it did. A miracle. On the 18th of September 2011, after years of trying, I got the opportunity to cover a show on 1Xtra. One whole show. I'd made it! Three hours of sitting in the 1Xtra studio and getting to talk into the hallowed 1Xtra mic. I was in Wonderland. Yes, it might have taken me a decade to get there – and copious amounts of emails with them telling me in no uncertain terms to bugger off – but it paid off in the end. And the first song I got to play? Rihanna's 'Cheers (Drink to That)'.

So, as you can see, those steps might be little, but as they add up, they pack a mighty punch. They give you so much momentum you become unstoppable. Even when you don't necessarily know what it is that you're moving towards, sometimes the universe will reward you with something even bigger than you could ever have dreamed up for yourself. On a Sunday night in 2015, 14 years after the disastrous Network X open day, I was asked if I'd like to present a show on 1Xtra's sister station – BBC Radio 1. Who'd have thought it? Definitely not me. I certainly didn't see that coming. It hadn't even occurred to me to hope to be on Radio 1; it seemed so far out of my league. It's like a footballer being asked to play for their country. But those small steps that I'd been taking had led me there. That little trickle of potential found its way and forged a path so great and wide that it led me to BBC Radio 1 – a station so big, you can hear it from space. Ha! It might have taken me nearly two decades to get there, but I did it; eventually I made it.

I so shouldn't have made it as a radio presenter. Don't get me wrong, I adored my time in radio. I am so grateful for every moment, minute and second I was able to sit in a studio, but I never felt like I belonged there. I always felt like a guest, like the luckiest listener who snuck in and joined the party for a while. I've always loved music and I've always understood the power of radio to bring people together. There's no other medium like it. It's magical. But I often wonder why I love it so much, especially when I spent most of my time there terrified and feeling like an imposter. I had to sit down a lot of the time because my legs would shake. I often couldn't eat before a show because I was sick with nerves. I had to write my words down so I wouldn't forget what to say. I remember one of my bosses meeting my little sister Lois. She'd come to work with me when she was about 11. She was super excited to be at my radio station and was being her usual brilliant, funny, confident self. My boss said she was a better presenter than me. He was right. It was plain for all to see. As much as it was hard for me to hear these things, and as much as I knew I'd never be the best, I never let it stop me trying my best. I always gave everything I had to each show. No matter how much my legs shook or my voice clammed up, I never gave up. I stuttered, stammered and found my way through, step by step, mistake by mistake, rejection after rejection. It's that cosmic course correction again. I didn't fear failure, I feared giving up. That's when you really fail. I couldn't do that – I loved music too much. I can't play music, I can't make music, I can't sing, I can't dance, I'm pretty rubbish at most things, to be honest, but there was something about radio that kept me going, kept me striving and, despite my fears, set my soul alight.

It's the connection, the community, the thought of the people you might be reaching, the people who might need to hear you that day. Radio was always there for me. No matter how odd or inadequate or weird I felt as a child, I could turn on the radio any time and be welcomed into its wonderful warmth, accepted with open arms. Every time I stepped into a studio, I hoped I was that friendly voice emerging through the ether, into the speakers, filling other homes with love and letting other people know they're not alone.

New Workout Plan

After I came out of hospital, I needed to adopt this same mindset of small, repeated actions leading to something bigger. I've always needed a purpose, something to work towards. Without anything to aim for, I flounder. I feel like a car with a broken satnav, aimlessly driving around, just trying not to crash! Once I was home after my surgery, it was important for me to fix my internal GPS and get back on the road to recovery. I needed a new routine for me and my backseat driver – Audrey – to follow.

Elaine the stoma nurse was on her way with some advice. It's always a joy to see Elaine. She makes me feel so relaxed, understood and, most of all, she understands the little monster that lives inside my pants. Elaine is like Audrey's fairy godmother, sprinkling her magic words and turning this little pumpkin into a princess. Kate and I welcomed Elaine into our home, all the while trying to study her face to see if we'd tidied up enough. Then it was down to my regular routine of pants-down-stoma-out (on the sofa this time) and time for a quick Audrey check-up. I gleefully obliged while Kate made the brews. Audrey, of course, behaved impeccably – she's a little charmer when she wants to be. Elaine set about doing her wonder work and stoma nurse midwifery – carefully observing the baby, checking she was healing OK, removing some of her stitches and giving her a general MOT which she passed with flying colours. Well done, Auds!

Elaine also advised me on the next steps for rehabilitating my body to help with the deep healing it still needed to do. Even though I felt stronger each day, I was still very slow on my feet and sitting up and lying down was tough on my torso. Keyhole surgery is a medical marvel; minimal surface clues on my body hide the deep level of trauma underneath. Considering what my body had been through, there wasn't much to see: a scar across my pelvis – which looks a bit like I've had a C-section – and various holes about the size of a pound coin stitched up and dotted around my tummy. I considered it my new art installation, the last remaining clues of my Big Bang – the blowing up and ballooning of my stomach cavity, stretching it far and wide to make the space needed to help the surgeons remove my tumour. Now I was left with my sun at the centre of it all – Audrey, my star – and behind her, a deep black hole leading back to the rest of my digestive system. So yeah, I guess I had quite a bit of healing to do. I had to remember to be patient and not rush to do physical things. I had to be mindful and practise self-care, which is not something that comes naturally to me. I knew I had to be sensible and listen to everything Elaine had to say. It's served me well so far. She's my stoma Yoda. She gave me some little goals to work towards, which was music to my ears.

Now, I'm not sure if the following advice varies from patient to patient, so please do check with your medical professional if you're going through something similar, but my new workout plan was ready:

- 20 minutes of exercise each day.
- Arnica: thought to help with healing and recovery.
- Lucozade Sport: an isotonic drink to help with dehydration and recovery.

That's it. Simple. These may have just been suggestions rather than instructions, but I really took the advice to heart. I had a feeling that these daily little wins would pay off big in the future.

I promised myself that I would start each day with an arnica tablet, make sure I drank a bottle of Lucozade Sport across the day and go on a little walk that would last about 20 minutes. I love walking and to me it's the next best thing to making me feel good if I'm not able to run. I'll be honest, I was very slow in the beginning. I was easily the slowest person on the pavement. I used to get rinsed by people with crutches and walking sticks. Kids used to look at me funny. I think they thought I was doing one of those races at school where you run in slow motion and try to be the slowest. Except I was shuffling, and quite often holding the right side of my body just in case anybody bumped into Audrey. I felt pretty fast and nippy when I was in the hospital, but on the big streets of London I was the tortoise and everyone else was the hare. I didn't care, I felt alive and it kept me motivated. It gave me purpose and a reason to get out of bed every day. Kate would help me and Audrey to get washed and dressed, then she'd pop us both out the door. I'd put on some good music and we'd get busy. It felt like I was telling every cell in my body that we were back. We were reclaiming ourselves from cancer. The bad cells were gone. Plus I knew that I was about to start a six-month course of chemotherapy, so I'd need to prepare my body as much as possible.

The walking got my blood pumping and kept my heart going. Most importantly, it got my head in the game and helped me visualise my body repairing itself. I imagined the holes on my body fusing back together again, the scar across my pelvis bonding shut, my muscles soaking up the arnica and Lucozade, powering up, my slow amble every day gently increasing in intensity and building momentum. My mind was being boosted by my music, my eyes were taking in the day, my skin was feeling the subtle changes in the weather and the temperature. I felt alive! I knew I wasn't promised this, but here I was. And I wouldn't waste another day; I wouldn't waste this second chance. I stuck to this new routine day after day, week after week. I was back in the game. The best game – this beautiful game of life!

My new regime paid off. I didn't want my treatment to slowly chip away at me and take me to a dark place. Lovely Ann and Maria, the nurses at the hospital, would tell me stories of people being on chemotherapy and still going to work. I'd also go on social media and see people continuing to work out or stay active, and it gave me such a boost. And, just five weeks after my surgery, on the 27th of November 2021, just before my chemotherapy started, I was back at Radio 1, back in the studio with my radio family and our gorgeous listeners.

I can't even begin to tell you how much I'd look forward to being at Radio 1 each weekend – music is the best medicine! Kate said sometimes I'd be so out of it in the mornings, she'd drop me off at Broadcasting House and it'd take me ages to shuffle across the plaza and into the John Peel wing. She said she'd watch me like a hawk until I disappeared through the door. But by the time she came back to pick me up, my shuffle had turned back into a walk, and I was smiling and full of beans. I was buzzing my bits off, babbling away and saying how much I'd enjoyed the show. If you tuned into those shows, I hope you know that you kept me going, you gave me a reason to dig deep and keep trying. You helped me stay being me.

When I woke up on the 1st of December, I realised what Kate had been spending her time doing while I'd been out on my walks. She'd put some of that tat of hers to good use and made Audrey an advent calendar – the incredible 'Audrobe' – containing 25 custom stoma bags, each with a different theme, taking us right up to Christmas Day. I turned to Kate and buried my head in her shoulder. I couldn't believe my luck: Kate, Elaine, my family, the NHS, Radio 1, our amazing listeners . . . Just how lucky I'd been to get cancer at this time, with these people to help me. I felt like I'd won the lottery.

NOTE TO SELF:
DREAM BIG, START SMALL.

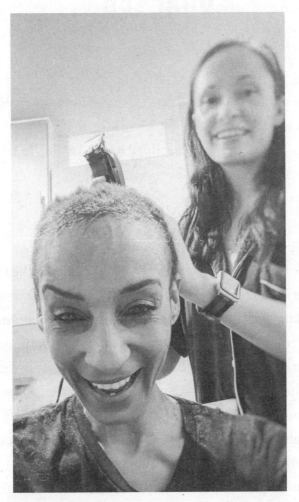

The Cure & The Cause
Fish Go Deep and Tracey K

CHAPTER 6

'By you I'm consumed.'

The Cure and The Cause

M e: 'Yeah, go on do it. Shave my head off.'
Kate: 'It's shave your HAIR off. Not your head.'

It was New Year's Eve 2021, and I was in the kitchen with Kate asking her to get me ready, get me into battle mode by shaving my hair. I was ready to cut off all that old energy and start 2022 with a literal clean head. I was a few weeks into chemotherapy and I was nervous. Not because of the chemo, but because I didn't know if I'd suit a shaved-off head. I suspected I might look like a potato. Good to know I was focusing on the important things in life.

I'd just begun six months of oral chemotherapy treatment. My pretty pink pills: Pentyl [1-(3,4-dihydroxy-5-methyl-tetrahydrofuran-2-yl)-5-fluoro-2-oxo-1H-pyrimidin-4-yl]carbamate or, as they're more commonly known, Capecitabine – their stage name! Even though I'd had surgery to remove my tumour, cancer cells could still remain, undetected. The chemo would get deep into my body and hopefully kill any bad cells that might be lurking. I'd had no idea I could take such powerful, cancer-busting poison in the comfort of my own home. I also had no idea that it was going to be the cause of so much physical pain. It ripped right through me. Nothing was left untouched or unaffected. It destroyed my sense of smell and taste. It turned my tongue black. It burned my skin, systematically dismantling my body and erasing my senses. You don't realise how much you appreciate these gifts in life until they are gone.

I'd been told that there was a good chance I wouldn't lose my hair with the drug I was on, but I was starting to notice its condition deteriorating and, besides, I'd already committed to my new hairdo, inspired by one of the ladies I spent time with in hospital. I wanted to help reclaim bald heads – they get such bad press, especially for women. I'd just seen a scene in *Game of Thrones* where the character Cersei has her hair shaved and is dragged naked through the streets by a nun ringing a bell and shouting *Shaaaaame!* as she goes. Well, the only bell I hoped to be ringing with a shaved head was the one at the end of chemo. Sometimes a shaved head can be a crowning glory . . .

Two Queens

Towards the end of my week in hospital after surgery we got new neighbours. Our little ward was starting to fill up. In the bed opposite mine to my left was a young woman who looked like she was in her early twenties. I didn't get to see her too much because her cubicle curtain was closed a lot of the time. Across from me to my right was another lady. She was maybe in her fifties and wore a cosy fleece jacket and beanie hat to keep her head toasty. I was new to all this and I didn't realise at first why she was wrapped up so warm. I hadn't begun that part of my journey yet. These magnificent ladies' lives are absolutely none of my business, but watching them helped and inspired me immeasurably. I hope they don't mind me sharing here the lessons I learned from them.

The younger lady to my left was very quiet. She quite often had nurses coming to check on her and doctors doing the same. I'm not sure, but I sensed that she was finding her time in hospital tough. But that's how she dealt with it – she'd stay in bed a lot, mostly with her curtains closed, and I rarely saw her. I made sure I was ready to give her a smile and catch her eye whenever I could. It wasn't until the stoma nurses had been to see me that she looked over. I smiled at her. Her face softened and she gave me a little smile in return before putting her head back on her pillow. I hope I brought her comfort with that little connection. She definitely made me feel less alone on that ward. Whatever was happening in her life at that moment, I felt, in that tiny smile, like she knew what I was going through. In that moment, we were the same. I still think about her to this day, and I hope wherever she is, she's doing OK.

The lady to my right was a little more forthcoming. She'd often be sitting on her bed, reading magazines, the papers or a book she'd brought with her. At other times, she'd be chatting away to friends and family on her phone, laughing heartily and remembering good times. She reminded me of my mum so much. You could tell she loved and missed her family, and her presence filled the ward with positive energy. She made me feel hopeful, and excited about seeing my mum again.

It wasn't until the next day that I found out a little more about her story. Two doctors came to visit her before she was due to be taken to surgery.

'Can we do anything for you?' they asked.

'Yes,' she said, 'can you take this cancer away from me?' She laughed as she said it, a defiant laugh that seemed to come from the depths of her soul. Her spirit would not be dampened.

She then went on to tell the doctors a bit about her story. She'd been to see her GP a few times with tummy problems. I'm not sure if it was the effect of Covid, general waiting times or if her symptoms had been missed, but by the time she'd been diag-nosed, it was too late. Her cancer was terminal, and she'd already had part of her stomach removed. She'd started chemotherapy, I think, to help shrink the tumour she was about to have taken away. I was completely in awe of her strength and spirit.

Just before she was due to go to surgery, she took off her warm jacket and removed her hat carefully, like she was lifting a crown. Her head was sore and scarred and bare due to the treat-ment she'd already received. She sat up on her bed, shoulders back, her head held high. Even though her cancer was termi-nal, even though her body was tired and cold and her head was bare, she looked so powerful – like a queen about to go into battle.

These are just two different examples of people coping with the unimaginable. There is no right or wrong way, only YOUR way. I think of those two ladies a lot. Both had their own way of dealing with what they were living through: a quiet determination and a bold, regal defiance. They were coping as best they could, in a way that made sense to them. I knew not to compare myself to anyone else, but I took inspiration and strength from them and used their examples to work out methods of my own.

New Year, New Me

I was now on Cycle 2 of chemotherapy, and my little pink soldiers were not holding back. They were running wild in the aisles. They'd gone full *Call of Duty* mode – expert level, headset and everything – ripping through my body and rearranging my face. When I looked in the mirror, I didn't recognise myself. It seemed I'd started the year with a free NHS facelift. I was swollen, puffy, and it looked like someone had given me a spray tan with a blow torch. I was absolutely botched! I looked like Madge off *Benidorm* if she'd been left out in the sun, strapped to a lounger for a week and had a few of her ciggies stubbed out on her face.

So chemo works then, I thought as I surveyed the damage.

Me: 'Do you think I should call the hospital and see if they can maybe tweak my medication?'

Kate nodded. She thought that might be best.

Just a quick reminder: everyone's experience with cancer and chemotherapy is different. I absolutely do not want this to put anyone off. I'll always remember my Auntie Ann (Dad's sister) saying, 'If they offer you chemo, take it.' I knew that I was lucky to have even been offered it in the first place. It's not a given. Chemotherapy is very expensive and, as I'm sure you've already gathered, it's powerful stuff – a potent poison that must be used with the utmost care and respect. Unfortunately for me, my skin was very sensitive to it, but a reduction of my dosage and a quick trip to the hospital dermatologist to get a few vats of various creams, and we were starting to at least soothe the burn. To be honest, I didn't care about the damage; I just didn't want to be taken off chemo. The thought of not doing everything I could to stamp out the cancer outweighed the side effects in my mind.

Of all of the side effects of chemotherapy, for me the most sinister one wasn't any of the painful physical symptoms; it was the insidious way it was slowly eroding who I was. It came for me like a thief in the night. It stole even the most simple of pleasures. It took away my comfort, the things that made me 'me'. I was fading. My favourite foods tasted of metal. My perfume made me feel sick. It robbed me of my facial features and it took away the one thing that we've universally accepted as our own unique calling card – my fingerprints. It sounds like science fiction, but chemotherapy really can make you lose your fingerprints – so much so that I lost the ability to use touchscreens. I remember trying to use a self-checkout in a shop, and my hands didn't register. As far as that till was concerned, I didn't exist. This moment hit me hard. I knew I had to find my way back. If I was going to get through this, I had to play chemotherapy at its own game. I wouldn't let it take away those things that make me who I am – I would use the very things that light me up to light my way out of this darkness. I remembered my lesson from those two ladies in the hospital, and I set about the business of being me. And whenever I don't feel like myself, there's only one thing for it – put on my trainers and run.

Running is my superpower – when I want to get into PB mode, it's the one I go for, no matter what I'm facing. It's my mobile medicine, meditation and manifestation tool all rolled into one. I didn't find running until later on in life – I was 37 when I started – but I'm so glad I did. What began as a shuffle morphed into running and eventually helped me get into the best shape of my life – mentally, physically and spiritually, the whole shebang. And what's even better, it's free! When I'm running I'm at my happiest, and it's my way of releasing all of my emotional energy.

So, during Cycle 2 of chemo, I took on a running challenge – RED January – where I ran a 5K every day during January. RED January is a fabulous annual running challenge designed to help with mental health alongside physical health. That year's motto was 'Moving Every Day, My Way'. *Perfect*, I thought. *Let's do it*. I pounded the streets, running for a different cancer charity every day with hope in my heart and a big, red, burnt-off face. What a way to start the year. The daily practice of looking forward to finding a new charity to support was a huge motivating factor for me. If you have a reason to run in your heart, you'll not only do it, it'll make you stupidly happy. Kate and I donated £5 for every 5K I completed. I was able to find and support 31 different cancer charities while recovering from cancer myself. Looking back at this challenge,

I don't know how I did it. It seems overwhelming to me now,
but at the time it made sense. I carried on being me. It might
not be running for you, it might be something else entirely that
lights you up, but whatever it is, make sure you keep doing it.
Keep that fire burning.

I guess I'd already decided in the hospital that I wasn't going
to take this lying down. I knew the moment I woke up from my
surgery that I would do everything I could to get my body in the
best place possible to deal with chemotherapy if I was offered it.
I focused on what I *could* control. I treated my body like a sav-
ings account. I saved a little bit every day – my own body bank.
I stocked up on good food, plenty of sleep, a 20-minute walk
with lots of gorgeous music to keep me happy. I got a routine in
place as quickly as I could and stuck to it. I continued going into
work at Radio 1 too. The only weekends I missed were due to
getting Covid. Chemo and Covid is not the one. If you can
avoid it, do. You don't want to earn that badge in the game of
life. Ha ha.

Every single step of those 5Ks felt amazing. I got to choose my
favourite music, the route I took, the beauty I saw through my
eyes, the things I thought about. I visualised the chemo pulsing
through my veins and kicking cancer's arse. The feeling of that
was so energising and powerful that I was able to complete
Bowel Cancer UK's 'Step up for 30' challenge during Cycles 6
and 7 of my treatment in April. Again, I completed a 5K every
day. I ran the ones I could, jogged others and walked or shuffled
the rest, but I still did it. It was my daily FU to cancer. And
thanks to the generosity of my family and friends and wonderful

PLAYLIST

Little
me

Tracklisting

Intro - 'Step by Step' - Whitney Houston
 - 'I Will Survive' - Gloria Gaynor
 - 'How Can You Mend A Broken Heart?' - Al Green
1/ - 'This Is Me' - Keala Settle
1/ - 'Rain On Me' - Lady GaGa + Ariana Grande
4/ - 'Make It Happen' - Live at MTV Unplugged - Mariah Carey
5/ - 'The Cure + The Cause' - Fish Go Deep + Tracey K
6/ - 'Listen' - Beyoncé
7/ - 'Let It Be' - The Beatles
8/ - 'Sometimes The Going Gets A Little Tough' - Finn
9/ - 'Have Yourself A Merry Little Christmas' - Judy Garland
10/ - 'Believe' - Ministers de la Funk + Jocelyn Brown
11/ - 'Gonna Fly Now' - Theme From "Rocky" - Bill Conti
12/ - 'Feet Don't Fail Me Now' - Jay Crookes
13/ - 'Finally' - Kings of Tomorrow feat. Julie McKnight
Outro - 'At Your Best' - Aaliyah
Acknowledgements + Thank Yous - Bonus Track -

Me, Mum and Smokey the dog.

Me in one of my many school uniforms.

Lesley, Diane and me doing body building like Uncle Tony.

Me and Lesley on Christmas Day, 1987. My first Walkman – I never took it off!

Me and Lesley

Lesley, Kameo and Me.

My Mum, my Nana and my Auntie Maxine.

Auntie Maxine & Uncle Tony.

My parents when they were younger.

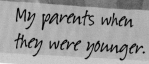

Mum and Dad - 2021.

Brothers and sisters, 1995 – back row, from left-to-right Loren, Lesley, me; front row Lloyd, Lois, Les Jnr.

Recreating our baby picture . . .

My Dad and his horse Ozzie on Southport beach.

My loves, Kate & my mum on Christmas Day, 2017.

Bloating – a symptom of bowel cancer. Taken on the day of my diagnosis 1 October 2021.

We love you, NHS!

Cheering and DJing for the runners at the London Marathon, 2021. Two days after my diagnosis.

Wearing my 'Today is a good day' t-shirt.

Elaine, my stoma nurse.

LUNCH
Patient Name Adele Roberts
Date 29/10/21   Diet
Ward T7   Bay/Bed 49
Starter clear soup
Main Course chicken + plain jacket potato
Dessert 42 with custard
Kosher   Halal   African Caribbean
Red Tray   Extra Gravy   Allergies Alert

SUPPER
Patient Name Adele Roberts
Date 29/10/21   Diet
Ward T7   Bay/Bed 49
Starter clear soup
Main Course chicken + plain jacket potato
Dessert 43 with custard
Kosher   Halal   African Caribbean
Red Tray   Extra Gravy

Before surgery: a plaster to protect Elaine's Sharpie work, waiting for surgery.

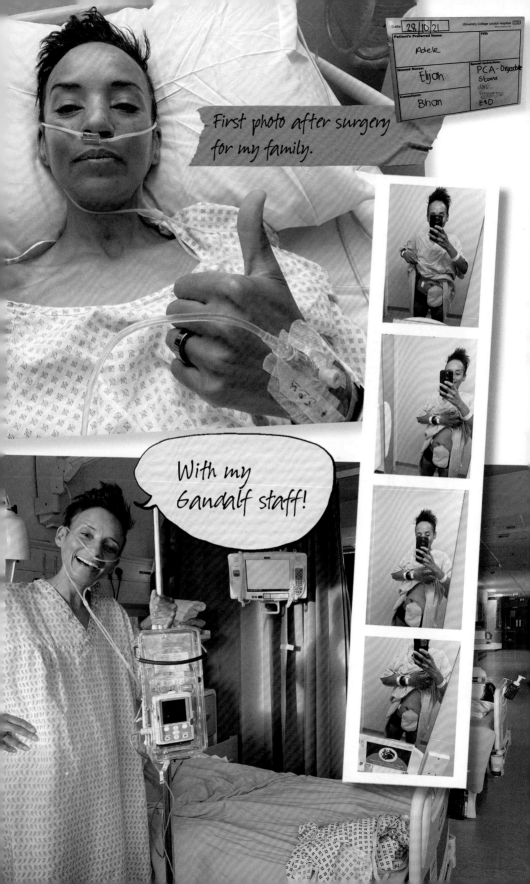

Meet Audrey!

The Audrobe!

people online, we raised over £5,000 for the charity. How amazing. Look what positive energy can do.

The Hard Yards

By the end of chemo, the skin on the soles of my feet and the palms of my hands was falling away. I had to wear cotton gloves to protect my hands from the damage. My feet were the worst. At first, the pain was intermittent. I'd be out doing my daily walk or shopping and the pain would just hit me out of nowhere. It was like a rubbish version of 'the floor is lava', but the lava wasn't on the floor, it was in my shoes, and I couldn't jump away from it, I couldn't escape. It was agony. Pain like that transforms your body. I'd be twisted, all bent over and shuffling home. It hurt so much it brought tears to my eyes. Kate did a bit of research on the internet and we found a lot of stories of people using Bag Balm and urea cream to help soothe the pain. They were amazing – my little pots of relief. I'd apply them at least three times a day and they helped so much.

I got severe morning sickness where I felt like I was out at sea on a booze cruise. The hospital was great and gave me domperidone (an anti-sickness medication) to help with the feeling. Kate also found these fabulous anti-sickness sweets called Queasy Drops to help. They were like magic. They stopped me feeling sick every time.

I also lost my body hair, and my skin went full Simpsons. I ended up a sallow grey/yellowish colour and, randomly, my tongue got big black spots on it. WTF?! It was patterned like a cow – a pink and black spotted cow, hiding in my mouth. Audrey started to suffer too. She was raging. She hated chemo, poor little love. I felt so sorry for her. Usually she's a rather perky pinkish colour. On chemo she was ultraviolet. Bright purple! She looked like Tinky Winky off the *Teletubbies* on acid (but without the handbag). She went all limp and barely moved. Usually she's dancing about and being cheeky. Not on chemo – she was gradually fading away too. Plus, Audrey had to deal with the toxic waste. Once the Capecitabine had raced around my body, it had to come out somewhere. That's the thing with a stoma: if you've put it in your mouth, it'll end up in your bag. The little pink pill turned into treacle-like toxic waste. The black stuff, we'd call it. It was vile, the stuff of nightmares. A poisonous oil slick just to top the whole thing off.

Morning sickness started my day and chemo dreams ruled the night, and the further into the treatment I travelled, the darker the nights became. My feet got so sensitive that they'd wake me up in the middle of the night. It felt like I'd been stabbed on my soles with a hot poker and I'd wake up to intense burning. I cannot even begin to tell you the pain. I had no escape, nowhere to run – I could barely walk. I slept downstairs alone so that I didn't wake Kate. She wanted to be there for me, but I didn't want the chemo to affect her sleep too. She was already doing an amazing job of nursing me during the day, and I wanted her to get some rest. That's the thing about cancer – it doesn't just affect you, it affects your family and friends too.

That's what hurt me the most in the early days – not hearing 'you have cancer' but having to tell my family and, out of everyone, having to tell my mum. I think that was the single most devastating moment of my life. How could I do that to her? After everything she's been through (and, believe me, she's been through it), it felt so unfair. When people ask me who's the most amazing person I've met, I might say someone famous because that's what most people expect, but deep inside I know it's my mum and dad. They are my heroes. End of. Growing up, inside our house, I felt safe. Outside, I learned very quickly that life isn't fair. On the great council estate game board of housing, there are way more snakes than ladders. And the ladders that are left will probably get robbed in the end anyway! It's wild. I can't even remember the number of different houses we lived in – we were picked up and plopped back down on a whim. There was one time my sister and I lived in a hostel with my mum. I'd been to seven different schools by the time I was eleven. It was chaotic, rough and ready – sometimes we had no money, there were wolves in sheep's clothing at every turn – but it was also an adventure. With my family, life was always exciting and full of love. I think that's the key. No matter what happened in life, I knew I'd always be OK because I had them. We are a team, and nothing will ever come between us. It hurt me so much to have to tell them my diagnosis. It was heartbreaking before a word had even left my mouth.

First up was my dad. He was a ledge, to be fair – proper stoic northern Dad. He made me feel like everything would be OK. He must have been worried; his sister had just been very ill with cancer and his brother-in-law had passed away from cancer.

Now his daughter was the current messenger and bearer. It must have been a shock to him, but he didn't let on. He said all the right things – he built me up and made me feel like, together, we'd all get through it. I felt much better about things. My dad gave me hope. I politely asked him not to tell anyone, especially my mum, because I wanted to tell her myself. He said OK. I don't think he was listening properly though, his mind must have gone into overdrive, because, within ten minutes, he'd told half of my family. He might as well have called the *Southport Visiter* and told them. He's a rascal!

I later asked my sister what had happened. Apparently he'd been standing next to my mum when I'd called him, so to avoid suspicion, he'd motioned to my sisters to go into the garden for a 'chat'. That made them go into overdrive. Instead of my sisters waiting to hear the sensitive nature of the news, they started guessing in their heads what it could be. One of them actually said to me, 'Dad was being dead weird, I thought he was going to say my boyfriend had been cheating on me.' I was on the other end of the phone thinking, No, *nothing that bad. I've just got cancer.* LOL. Then in a different conversation, my other sister said, 'I was so scared, I thought Dad was going to make me sell my dogs.'

I know it sounds weird, but it made me laugh so much. I think we were all so shocked that all of this confusion was actually very amusing. It made it less scary for all of us. I'm so glad we laughed instead of cried – and, let's face it, at least Loren didn't have to sell her puppies. They're so cute! We even share the same puppy pads (they're much cheaper than the ones for humans). Loren gave me a link to them on Amazon, and I use them to save me from Audrey's leaks.

The hardest part was telling my mum. That broke my heart. FU, cancer, for making me do it. I never wanted to speak its name anywhere near her. I didn't want its bad energy around her. I was so scared that day, my knees were shaking. My mum is not very well. Both my mum and Loren have a genetic condition called Spinocerebellar Ataxia Type 2 that progressively gets worse. It's all-encompassing and slowly works away at their body. It affects their movement, speech, motor skills and communication. There's no cure for it. It's devastating, it's cruel, but they are both so strong – they're my heroes. My health worries are nothing compared to what they face day after day. I will never complain about having cancer. Life's been good to me. They are the real reason I know how lucky I am. They're my proof. They're my example. They get up day after day and make the best of it. They're unreal. How could I ever complain when I have them on my team?

Mum's body and mind are greatly affected. Her condition and the medication to treat it make her shake pretty much all day long. It has turned a vibrant, voluptuous, incredible, beautiful woman into a tiny little frame. But she's so strong. She's been transformed physically and mentally, but being near her, I know she's still there. She's still our mum. That made all of this so much harder. I slowly walked up to her, knelt by her chair and put my hands on hers. I couldn't look her in the eye. I just held on to her as tightly as I could.

'Mum, please don't worry. I've got to have an operation soon. I've got a bit of a problem with my tummy and they need to fix it. I think it's a little lump. Don't worry, they've told me they can get it. I think it might be cancer, but at least they've found it early so I've got a good chance.' I finally looked up at her; her body was shaking from her condition.

She looked at me and said, 'OK.' And that was it. I squeezed her hands, stood up and hugged her as much as her fragile body would allow. She sat quietly, still shaking, but I knew inside she had heard what I had said. She knew what it meant. She was amazing. She was staying strong for me. It was taking all her strength just to exist. She's my hero, my inspiration. At least I had options and an opportunity for treatment. There is no cure for Mum's condition. Despite my news, I was the lucky one. Her condition is so cruel. It's slowly erasing her from the inside out, but to her credit, her spirit still shines through. My mum has become my biggest mentor, my greatest teacher.

Focus on the Positive

During chemo, Kate was amazing. At night, she'd get painkillers out of the blister packs for me and screw the tops off my water bottles before she went up to bed. If she didn't, I'd have to open the bottles with my teeth because I couldn't use my hands – they were that sore. I'd try to shuffle to get the painkillers, but my feet were so painful that the carpet felt like an attack, like a thousand angry knives stabbing my soles. I was being tormented by a carpet. I was afraid of the big shaggy pile. I couldn't wear shoes or sliders because putting anything on my feet hurt even more. The worst nights were when Audrey would chip in too. She'd wake me up, spraying her toxic waste all over me and my water-proof bedsheets. Well, I say 'bedsheets', my washable bed protectors and my big white and blue puppy training pads. So up I'd get again, cross the carpet of a thousand knives and go up to the bathroom to change my stoma bag at 2am with gloves on, feeling like my hands and feet were on fire. Oh and then change my pyjamas, change all my bedding and put a wash on. FM actual L!

I'd had enough. I was a mess. I was a rotting shell. My body was falling apart around me. *Why? Why is this happening to me? What have I done? Why am I being punished?* I'd lie in bed, hurting, trying to make sense of it all. There wasn't much positive thinking in those moments I can tell you! But eventually the painkillers would kick in, I'd calm down and I'd try to refocus. I did a lot of thinking on those nights, a lot of soul-searching. To me, positive thinking isn't really about being happy all the time, putting a smile on it and pretending everything is OK. It's about allowing myself to feel the hurt or the sadness or the disappointment, but also letting it go. As you've heard, I used to either hold on to feelings or ignore them and let them fester inside me. I'm trying to be better at that. I'm trying to allow myself to feel my emotions, but just know that, eventually, I'll start to come out the other side. I try to find the positives. That's what positive thinking is to me – focusing on the good.

My body might have been suffering physically, but my mind was in a better place because I made it so. I focused on all the good in life, everything I could think of to be grateful for. Every breath and every step, every time I got to wake up, every time I got to see my Kate. We made it our mission to appreciate each day, say thank you and go again. We did it together. We walked right through the fire! *Sings* *Through the fire, through whatever, come what may!* Yes, Chaka.

If I can feel, I'm alive. I'm lucky, I get to experience this. It's a privilege. This too shall pass. Nothing lasts forever, good or bad. My body might have been hurting, but my heart was full of hope and my mind was free. No matter what was happening to me physically, I wouldn't give up spiritually. Cancer and chemotherapy couldn't touch me. That was my victory.

The mind is stronger than the body.

Whatever you're facing in life, whatever your challenge, you get to choose where your focus goes, what you give energy to. Keep remembering who you are and do what lights you up the most. That's how you'll stay strong mentally. I didn't want to focus on the downsides of the treatment and I definitely didn't want to give cancer any more of my time. I was in charge now and I was taking my power back!

Every little step, each micro-movement, any positive thought, I knew it all counted. I imagined it helping me turn the tables of fate, allowing the odds to always be in my favour. I didn't worry about what life had in store for me, I just did what I could, with what I had, where I was at. I didn't hide from the incoming storm; I used its power to propel me on.

You can batten down the hatches
or you can learn to fly!

I'll be honest; it was tough. It really hurt. Chemotherapy stole my physical features and zapped my spirit. I was like a ghost – I was fading. In a lot of ways, it was worse than the cancer. Some nights I didn't even know if I could carry on. But I just kept going and kept my eyes on the finish line. Eventually I got to the other side. I did it my way.

NOTE TO SELF:
THERE IS NO RIGHT OR
WRONG WAY. THERE IS ONLY
YOUR WAY.

Listen
Beyoncé

CHAPTER 7

'Listen to the sound from deep within.'

Listen

We were on the TV! Kate, Audrey and I were gassed. It was January 2022, and it was our maiden voyage on the fabulous *Good Morning Britain*. The wonderful Kate Garraway (who I'll call Kate G for the next bit of the story so we don't mix her up with my Kate), Ben Shephard and the *GMB* team had kindly invited us on to the show to talk about our journey and to raise awareness of bowel cancer. How amazing is that? I never take it for granted when a show as big as *GMB* is willing to share its platform and busy schedule in order to help others. Not only was our appearance on the show a good way to remind viewers of the symptoms of bowel cancer, but it was also a chance to celebrate ostomates and an opportunity for me to get out of the house and carry on living my life while on chemo. Champion! That was so important to me. It was helping to motivate me and keep me going.

Since I'd been diagnosed, there had been so many people who had helped me, both online and in real life, so it made me incredibly happy to be able to play my part too. I was also thrilled that they invited Kate (my Kate) to join me on their sofa. Friends and family can often be forgotten in the furore of cancer. I hoped that Kate could help any other partners or family and friends who were going through it too. We're all in this together, and Kate and my family were the reason I kept believing I'd be OK. I'm so grateful that our little team was on the sofa – me, Kate and Audrey – because you never know who's watching or who needs to see you that day. Always remember you're not alone . . . and I hope somehow we helped.

Kate G and Ben are so good at their jobs – I could watch them work all day. It was like watching the Apple TV series *The Morning Show*. Kate G is Jennifer Aniston, and Ben is Steve Carell. Actually, let's make Ben Reese Witherspoon because Steve Carell's character is a bit, well, a bit cheaty . . . and Ben Shephard is so not cheaty.

Watching them segue expertly between politics, various news stories, 'headlines just in', lighter bits of entertainment and sensitively highlighting a subject as serious as cancer was an absolute masterclass. They did it all with aplomb, all while having a director chatting in their ear, looking flawless and keeping their cups of tea and half-eaten breakfasts just out of shot of the cameras. We were all aboard the good ship *GMB* and I was in awe.

Kate G, you are the real deal. I hope you don't mind me saying it, but you are a G. Since the *I'm a Celebrity* jungle, both of our lives have been hit by a thunderbolt from the blue and sent us independently headlong onto new paths. Seeing how Kate G has played the cards life has dealt her is magnificent. I'm not surprised though. She's a warrior. She was a force in that jungle. What a woman. She built the camp a drying rack – for our pots and pans – out of jungle vines, branches and trunks pretty much as soon as we moved in. With her bare hands! She got up every morning ready to take on the day, with a big smile on her face, willing to muck in. I don't remember her ever complaining. She's got the patience of a saint too. I guess that's being a mum for you. You're made of tough stuff ladies – I applaud you.

Kate G spoke about her husband Derek and her children all the time, and her face would light up when she did. So much so that when I got chucked out of camp and arrived back at the hotel, I knew who her family were as soon as I set eyes on them, even though I'd never met them before.

OK, let's rewind a little to 2019 and my time in the *I'm a Celebrity* jungle. I don't want to ruin the magic of TV, so I shall try to tread very carefully. I also don't want to get sued, so we'll see what the lawyers leave in here . . .

First of all, reality TV is not real. Put it this way: the first day we got in there, I heard one of the rocks sneeze. Those camera people can hide in holes and places that you wouldn't imagine. Bits that are true: Ant & Dec are bloody lovely (as were my campmates. I felt very lucky). Yes, you're hungry, the red telephone box only accepts incoming calls (we checked) and they absolutely do lower your food down to you in a sack. Oh, and you really do have to keep that fire going. You have to boil the water in order to drink it – you know, just so you don't get diarrhoea or die – and even though you're not technically in the jungle (you're in the bush), everything either bites you or has the ability to kill you (campmates not included). Oh, and one final thing: hearing the name 'Dec' in an Australian accent will make you laugh every time. Ha ha.

I originally thought that the first signs of my cancer started to show a couple of years after *I'm a Celeb*. I was wrong. It was there for us all to see in the camp, but we didn't know – not even Dr Bob, who works on the show to keep everyone safe. I am absolutely not blaming anyone by the way, but maybe if I'd have been more aware of the symptoms I could have asked for help earlier. Plus, as good as Dr Bob is, he doesn't have a colonoscopy machine in his jungle hut, or permission to touch my bum for that matter, so there's nowt he could have done.

'You look like you're dead when you're asleep.' I can't tell you how many times my campmates said this to me. We used to laugh about it all the time. I also used to find it very hard to stay awake once the sun had gone down. It was like my body would lose power with the light. I think I was always first in bed. There was one night I got so cold that I couldn't even stay up for our food. I put on every piece of clothing that I had. We had two versions of everything and I wore it all, including my coat, and I kept my boots on. I climbed into bed and just shut down. My campmates were so worried about me. Kate, who was watching at home, knew there was something wrong too. I would never go to bed without having my tea. She rang one of the producers to say she was worried. They said I was just a bit cold and tried to put her mind at rest.

It scares me thinking about it now. I didn't know it at the time, but I was ill with bowel cancer. I've since asked my surgeon about my tumour and he said it had probably been growing for at least ten years. The hospital found it at a scan in September 2021 – I was in the jungle in December 2019 ... that's scary.

I also couldn't eat my food. I think I was the only campmate in the show's history to not eat the rations. It hurt my tummy and I had no appetite anyway. I used to eat what I could and then give the rest to James Haskell. He bloody loved eating my food! Ha ha. Dr Bob was worried about me when he heard I was off my food, so they fed me nutrition shakes in secret, and I had to be weighed regularly, but the pounds were falling off me. The producers urged me not to share my TV food and to eat it. I tried the best I could, but I either wasn't interested or it hurt too much. Luckily, I got to do a lot of eating challenges. For some reason, my appetite was better in the daytime so, in a way, thank God for the turkey testicles and camel toes. I think they actually saved my life!

So just to reiterate: loss of appetite, a sore, bloated tummy, weight loss and fatigue. These are the classic symptoms of bowel cancer, and they were playing out on TV for all to see. I'm also even more grateful now that I was chucked off first. That might have saved my life too. I was dying and I didn't know it.

Jump to summer 2021 and I started to see mucus whenever I'd go to the toilet. My appetite had recovered from *I'm a Celeb* and I'd put a little bit of weight back on, but I was still quite slender. I seriously thought it was just because I enjoyed running. I felt like I was in the best shape of my life. How could I be ill? I didn't *feel* ill. Over time, the mucus started to occasionally have blood in it. Not a lot of blood, but enough for me to notice. Then the blood didn't go away. I told Kate:

'It's because you eat so much kale and you don't cook it properly.'

We laughed, I agreed, and that was it. Unbeknown to me, that was the final piece of the pie. The other main symptom of bowel cancer: blood in your poo. I didn't think too much of it, but as the weeks progressed and the blood kept appearing, I remembered a call from my dad. He'd noticed blood in his poo a few years earlier and he'd been worried. He asked for my advice. I couldn't believe it. Not only was my dad asking *me* for advice, but he was also considering going to the doctor's. You could have knocked me over with a feather. His head could be falling off and he'll try to soldier on. I think he even fixed his own broken leg once. He's a nightmare. But to be fair to him, he went to the doctor's and got checked out. It had made me so proud, and luckily, after doing some tests, his symptoms were nothing to worry about. I thought, *Well, if my dad can do it, I can too.*

I'll be honest, I didn't call the doctor's straight away. I googled a bit, thought it was probably piles or IBS – or kale like Kate said – and left it at that. Nice one, Dr Adele. I didn't want to burden the NHS because it was still dealing with the aftershocks of Covid and I didn't want to waste anyone's time, but as the weeks went on and the blood-mucus weirdness didn't stop, I decided to call. It took about six weeks to get an appointment – an appointment that would save my life. Thank you, Dr Yuen. I told Dr Yuen my symptoms and she asked politely if she could examine me. Kate was there to hold my hand through it all. Dr Yuen checked my bottom and said she thought it was piles. She said I was too young for it to be anything like bowel cancer BUT she'd give me some tests to check anyway, just to be on the safe side. Imagine if she hadn't made that decision or shown that duty of care. It doesn't even bear thinking about. I still shudder at the thought. There are so many people who either don't go to their GP or *do* go and see their GP and are told they are too young and aren't offered a test. I was so lucky. There was a 6 per cent chance that it would be bowel cancer for me as I'm under the age of 50. I thank my lucky stars every day that my tumour was found and was still treatable.

'Life whispers to you all the time. And if you don't get the whisper, the whisper gets louder. I call it like a little pebble, a little thump upside your head. You don't pay attention . . . the problem becomes a brick.'
– Oprah Winfrey

Please request a FIT if you're worried – and seek a second opinion if you're not happy. Ask your GP to rule out cancer FIRST. And when it comes to symptoms, please just let me say this: I've been there; I've been that person who doesn't want to find a lump or a bump. I used to think I'd rather not know. I see it differently now. Symptoms are a blessing in disguise. They're your body's way of saying it needs help. They show up to help us. Ignoring your symptoms is like having a smoke alarm, hearing it go off and then taking out the batteries. IT'S STILL GOING OFF, YOU JUST CAN'T HEAR IT. Get those batteries back in and work out if it's a false alarm or if there's a fire. And if it is a fire, don't let it rip through your whole house. Get help.

Don't fear the warning signs, fear ignoring them.

Bowel cancer is the fourth most common cancer in the UK but the second biggest killer – second only to lung cancer. It's also one of the most treatable forms of cancer. If it's found early enough, you can be treated. Every time you go to the toilet is a chance to check. If any of this resonates with you or it's making you worried for someone else, please seek help. You'll never have a better chance than today to get it diagnosed and to beat it. Please don't leave it too late. I don't want this terrible disease to take any more of us or hurt any more of our loved ones. If we all look out for each other and ourselves, we can stop it ruining more lives.

Main symptoms of bowel cancer
- *Bleeding from your bottom and/or blood in your poo.*
- *A persistent and unexplained change in bowel habit.*
  - *Unexplained weight loss.*
- *Extreme tiredness for no obvious reason.*
  - *A pain or lump in your tummy.*

Source: Bowel Cancer UK

OK, hopefully that's helped. That's the only bit in the book where I'll try to tell you what to do. Please get help if you're worried. The world is a better place with you in it.

Now let's continue . . .

NOTE TO SELF:
LISTEN TO YOUR GUT. THE ANSWERS ARE WITHIN.

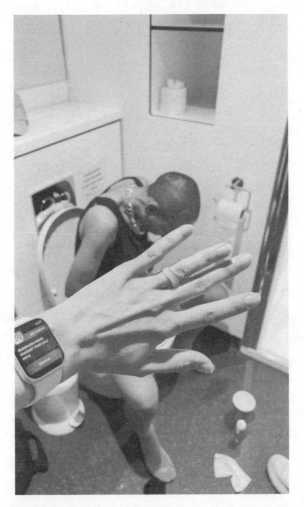

Let it Be
The Beatles

CHAPTER 8

'When I find myself in times of trouble.'

Let It Be

May bank holiday 2022 would be a collection date to remember – the start of Cycle 8 and the final batch of Capecitabine to pick up from the chemist. Only two more weeks of pilling and purging, downing my pretty, pink poison and stomaching its vommy side effects. I couldn't wait!

For the past six months, my life had been 'two weeks on, one week off' – half a year of taking three pills twice a day and riding the rollercoaster of chemo. As much as I was grateful for the ultimate white-knuckle ride, it was about to come to an end, and I was relieved. I was ready to get off. I was more than green about the gills – my gills were black and dropping off. I hoped I'd never have to visit this funfair again. I strapped on my big, boaty trainers and braced myself: one more dig for victory!

We began our quest to the hospital – our hospital on the hill. I shuffled and Kate patiently walked alongside me. We talked about what we'd been through and imagined how good we'd feel when this stage was over. Each thought helped fuel our steps, helped power us along our ever-rising path. I was exhaust-ed, but I'd psyched myself up. After all we'd been through, all those dark days and fiery nights, I was so proud of myself for walking to the final pick-up. Eventually, we caught sight of the hospital. We excitedly made our way to reception, put on our Covid masks and headed for the stairs. Usually we'd be treated to an escalator ride, but today it was broken. We didn't care. We skipped up that staircase like Ginger Rogers and Fred Astaire. This was it, the moment had arrived. My lungs were heaving from the mini masked workout, but my painkillers were keeping my fiery feet at bay. We knew what awaited us – the pharmacy; our glorious destination. Bring on the dealers, the pharmacists, the dispensers of my life-saving pink pills. We turned to our right annnnnnnnddddd . . . nothing.

Nowt.

Chuff all.

No queue, no lights, no friendly faces, no hustle and bustle – just silence and a load of impenetrable, white metal shutters. The hospital pharmacy was closed. FFS. We asked a passing member of staff.

'They don't do bank holidays,' we were told.

'Oh.'

Kate and I looked at each other. We stood there for a moment, each drew in a breath, thought on it, took a beat and had a little smile. Kate motioned to me, 'Come on'. I nodded and obliged. I manoeuvred my heaving, aching body to the stairs and we began the slow, bumbling descent back down. So much had happened since I was diagnosed with cancer that the pharmacy situation didn't bother me. It didn't even touch the sides. These things happen. Plus, all in all, I was washed, dressed and I'd done my daily walk. Today was a good day, and the bonus of going to the hospital is that you pass Aldi on the way home. Result! As pressing as my treatment was, I could wait another day. *It's not going to kill me!* I thought (well, I hoped). So off we went, back down the hill, had a little scoot around Aldi and a quick trip to pick up Kate's dry cleaning. That'll do for me.

> *'If you are irritated by every rub, how will you be polished?'*
> – Rumi

This whole journey has taught me to expect nothing, but to appreciate everything. There's an old proverb (and also a Public Enemy album) that says, 'Man plans, God laughs', and it's so true! It's helped me become more mindful, to live in the moment and to be less attached to an 'outcome'. I used to hold such a tight grip on how I thought things had to go and had to be. Usually, this turned into me swimming against the current and trying to force square pegs into round holes. Now, I try to go with the flow and appreciate wherever it takes me.

Amor fati – here come those wise Stoics. It's a good one this one. A hard one to get your head around at first, but if you can do it, it's the gift that just keeps on giving. Amor fati means 'love fate'. I wanted to get it tattooed on my knuckles but my mum said no (gutted – it would fit perfectly too).

Love fate. Love what happens. All of it. Everything. The

whole life-shaped pie. Good or bad. Come what may. It's like having the best pair of glasses through which to view the world.

Don't get me wrong, it's hard. I have to remember to employ this mindset a lot (hence the desire to have it tattooed on me), but when I can do it, it's bliss. It's pretty much saying that, yes, life's a shit show, but you knew that already. Know that some of it will be bad, horrendous even, but always remember this too shall pass. You'll get to the other side and you'll be stronger for it.

Everything that happens to you in life is an opportunity to grow.

Amor fati helped me change my perspective during the darkest days of my diagnosis and treatment. It helped me reframe things and see them from a different angle – it still does. When I started to let go of how I believed things should be, I actually started to become happier. I became more balanced, more chill. It's tiring trying to control life and wishing things were different. I let go. I surrendered. I went with the flow of life instead of against it. This way of thinking also helped keep my spirits up when I later found out that my hilly hospital didn't have an end-of-treatment 'celebration bell'. I wouldn't get to hear it ring after all; just the sound of me asking Kate if she could open my water bottle, while a bald, burnt and gloved me tried to chug enough water to swallow my final portion of poison. Now that's a season finale!

I didn't get a nice shareable end-of-treatment photo of me triumphantly ringing a shiny, golden bell, but that's OK. I got through it – I made it to the other side and was so happy to start living my life again. I was back in the game, with hope in my heart and a raging bull in my pants. A bovine beast named Audrey. I feel like she's already had some good shout-outs in our journey so far, but I might just mention a couple more before we proceed. Plus it's all about balance: I can't just sing her praises; I also need to tell you when she's been a little horror. If Audrey has taught me anything, it's to expect the unexpected. When I make plans, Audrey laughs . . .

Audrey's Greatest Hits

I think I've said it before, but I'll say it again: gut reaction is real. Like, *really* real. I know this might sound a bit wild, but I've seen mine in action. Audrey is part of my parasympathetic nervous system – a network of nerves that subdues and relaxes our bodies after periods of stress and danger. It also encompasses the parts of our body that move and work away in the background, helping to keep us alive. If they didn't do this, we wouldn't fare too well. Imagine having to consciously make your heart beat, or your liver detox, or your stomach digest. I struggle to remember what day it is sometimes; I'd be dead within the hour. *How did she die again? She forgot to breathe.* Yep, I'd be dead in five minutes flat. Any strong emotion from me and Audrey moves. I didn't notice this in hospital because I didn't really have the chance to speak to her. I might have thought about her in my mind, but I didn't speak to her out loud. I mean, that would have been a bit weird – me, alone in the hospital, sitting talking to a stoma bag. I'm not sure they would've let me out! But, when I got her home, all that changed. If I hear music I like, Audrey dances; if Kate talks, she swoons; if I talk, she moons . . . I don't think she likes me very much. I'm merely her vessel of being. She thinks I'm an idiot. I'm Pinky and she's The Brain. So much for the gut being the second brain – Audrey thinks she's in charge. I'm the sous-chef in this kitchen and Audrey is the Gordon Ramsay, and when she feels like it, she unleashes hell's kitchen.

We've already talked a bit about my very unhelpful habit of burying my emotions. I bury them like parents bury our old pets. Yep, talk about *Pet Sematary* – my back garden is full of them (metaphorically, of course). That movie put me off having pets for life. I still got one in the end though, didn't I? Audrey – my little mini beast, my terroriser and tormentor, but also my life-saving mentor. Maybe it's a blessing in disguise that I can see my feelings – my subconscious, the thoughts and habits that drive me. I'm more mindful now. I have to be. If I'm getting too nervous or stressing about things too much, Audrey goes wild in the aisles. It's grounding. When this happens, it's time to take notice. Nerves and excitement seem to be her big triggers. I used to quite enjoy butterflies before, now they're a warning sign that Auds is about to make a run for it . . .

The shower scene

Psycho anyone?! This was the first night after coming home from the hospital. Kate and I decided to attempt our first stoma bag change, and Audrey decided to go full Norman Bates on us. It was quite the couple's night in. To our horror, we quickly realised that we were a couple no more. We were now a *throuple*, and the Audster was in charge.

Audrey fucked us up that night. We took off her bag and she wouldn't go back in. Every time Kate went near her, she'd spray us like a demon hosepipe. I must have drunk too much water or something, but that little sucker didn't tire for hours. It was brutal. Plus my body was still beaten up from surgery and I had stitches everywhere. I could barely stand up, let alone catch a naughty stoma in a bag. Never mind ringing the hospital for help, I thought we were going to have to ring the police and get her arrested. It was bad. Kate started crying. I did too, from the pain. I thought it was never going to end. Audrey was like a super soaker. She absolutely destroyed the bath mat. She went all up Kate's arm, on the walls. Kate shouted for me to *get in the shower!* I had to stand in there until she stopped. I thought I was going to pass out. It was too much. We were like The Chuckle Brothers: *to me, to you*. We didn't have a clue. We *were* The Chuckle Brothers, but with no jokes. It was tragic. We eventually managed to wrangle Audrey into a bag, but it was a complete baptism of fire.

Getting loose for *Loose Women*

Audrey loves MILFs. She's also very fond of the Loose Women. Like REEAAALLLLY fond. It was the day after my last dose of chemo and what better way to mark the occasion than a trip to *Loose Women*? YES! Can you believe it? I got to go to the place where daytime queens are made. I was honoured. And I got a great line-up too: Christine, Coleen, Janet and Jane (not Jane McDonald – she's left the show to go cruising, but that's probably a blessing in disguise because I would have lost my mind even more if she'd have been there). I was in my element. I'd gone on with a view to hopefully help raise awareness of bowel cancer and to celebrate the fabulous world of being an ostomate. A dream day – little old me and Audrey sitting in the middle of four fabulous women.

I think the thought of that and Audrey's penchant for hotties set her off. Any intense emotion brings about motion in the ocean. I'd tried to make an effort – Kate had bought me a lovely pink suit. I was backstage and it was nearly time to get dressed and make my way up to the studio. Audrey had other plans. The TikTok of this moment has been viewed over two million times. Anyway, back to my pink suit. I thought it would complement the *Loose Women* set nicely and maybe zhuzh up my chemo chic look a bit. I hoped anyone watching at home who might be starting chemo would get a little boost seeing it and know it was going to be OK. I hoped they would see past the chalky, sallow skin I was currently wrapped in. I hoped my happiness inside would shine through. Yes, I looked like death warmed up, but inside I was buzzing . . . and Audrey was scheming.

She took her chance. At the exact time I was told to start getting ready to go to the studio, Audrey decided to kick off her bag and get naked. I felt her striptease immediately. She started to dance. I made a run for it and began a striptease of my own. Me versus Audrey: which one of us could take our clothes off the fastest? Audrey was using last night's tea and the last few dregs of the chemo pills to break her way out of her stoma bag prison. I tried to pull my posh pink suit trousers down as quickly as I could, but I had those bloody chemo gloves on, and my hands wouldn't work. I screamed for help. *KATE! COME QUICK, SHE'S GETTING ME!* Kate knew the drill. She ran across the dressing room like she was in a scene from *Baywatch*.

'Quick, get some tissues!'

The bag had no chance; Audrey was too powerful – it was pretty much off. Kate did what she could, got Audrey in a tissue headlock and cut off her flow. I kicked off my pants and strad- dled the toilet like a big, bloated, squatting duck. There was a knock at the dressing room door.

'We're ready for you!'

It was time to go to the *Loose Women* studio and I was naked from the waist down with my girlfriend holding my stoma in a piece of tissue. FOLs.

'Just a minute!' we said. 'We'll be there in a sec. Please don't come in!'

It. Was. Carnage. I was mortified. Kate had to go out and explain what had happened. We've learned to just tell the truth with things like this now and not worry about it. And, to be fair, most people are totally lovely and understanding. Kate even managed to get me some spare pants from the wardrobe depart- ment that belonged to Jane Moore from the panel. I don't think to this day she knows I had her pants on while we calmed Audrey down and tidied up, LOL.

It ended up being a great day, and the Loose Women were just as lovely and dreamy as you'd imagine. As soon as we got in the studio, Audrey was a little treasure. She's such a kiss ass. Even though they're all my faves, Janet Street-Porter made me laugh so much. She told me during the break, 'Thank you for coming on to talk about bowel cancer today. I did a FIT test once. I forgot about it and walked around with shit in my bag for a week. I totally forgot to post it.' So that's what happens while the commercials are on? Ha ha. She's too funny. She's also a ledge and has given me the perfect chance to remind you: if you're offered a FIT, please do it. They're so easy to do – it takes less than two minutes, and you'll be going to the toilet anyway. Don't be shy, give it a try! That little pot might just save your life.

We don't talk about Audrey's prolapse

This one was like a stress dream. There was a lot going on that day. It's August 2022 and the day of Scott Mills's final radio show on BBC Radio 1 – the final day of a glorious 28-year impeccable career. I adore Scott Mills. I'd been listening to him long before I joined the BBC and have always marvelled at his prowess, his mastery of radio, his diction. If you ever get the chance to sit in the studio and see Scott work, take it! To be honest, I don't know if he actually offers 'sit-in' sessions; I just bugged him until he said yes.

So, as you can imagine, his final show on Radio 1 was an EVENT. All the presenters had been invited into Radio 1 to celebrate with Scott and Chris Stark (Scott's co-presenter) after the show. I wanted to be there with all my heart. I'll be honest with you, I'm a bit shit when it comes to social gatherings – especially goodbyes. I don't like goodbyes. In fact, I don't *do* goodbyes. With Scott, though, I was ready to have a word with myself, keep my anxiety at bay and kiss the ring of the king. That's how much he means to me. He is a mentor, an inspiration, an incredible person and someone I'm so proud to call my friend.

So, I'm freaking out about going to his party, oh and later on that night I'm going to be presenting a show on BBC Radio 2, covering for Jo Whiley, another radio icon. So no pressure there then? Basically, I'm bricking it about the whole day.

Kate knew I'd be climbing the walls so she was kind enough to accompany me on my daily walk. We decided to go to King's Cross. It's a lovely walk over there from our house. We get to stroll along the canal and be around fancy shops and lots of purposeful people, whether they're about to make a journey, go on a trip of a lifetime or go to college – the great Central Saint Martins university is there. King's Cross has got good energy – forward momentum. I love it. Plus there are lots of toilets so it's the perfect place for me.

I had a bit of a tummy ache that day. Something didn't quite feel right, but I didn't want it to stop me. We were about 15 minutes into our amble when I started to get a dull, persistent, heavy pain in my tummy. It felt a bit like period pain. I didn't get periods when I was on chemo, so I thought it must have been a phantom one. I carried on walking. Then came a succession of sharp pains that made me double over.

Kate: 'Are you OK?'

Me: 'My tummy's really sore today, but let's carry on. I think I can walk it off.'

We carried on all the way to King's Cross station. I bought some painkillers to help with the pangs, but I knew it was something more serious than usual. I just couldn't seem to shake it off.

Me: 'I'm so sorry, Kate, I know we've only just got here, but do you mind if we get the bus back? I don't feel well.'

Kate didn't mind at all. She was worried. So off we went, back home on the bus. My stoma bag felt weird. It was massive by the time we got home. I wondered what the hell was in it. It felt heavy.

'I'm going to change my bag,' I said to Kate, making my way to the bathroom. 'Will you put the radio on so we can hear Scott's last show?'

On went the radio and into the toilet I went. I took off my bag and I couldn't believe what I saw. Audrey, who's usually the size of, let's say, a baby carrot, had exploded and was now the size of a baby elephant trunk. I'm not kidding. She was so big and heavy that gravity had kicked in. As I slowly pulled off my bag in disbelief, Audrey unravelled like a python. It was disgusting. She ended up hanging by my knee. WT actual F?

'Audrey, are you OK? Is that you?'

This wasn't a stoma; it was a whole intestine. It was unbelievable. There was no way that was going back in. I panicked. I didn't know what to do. I didn't want to tell Kate – she was going

to kill me; I'd been walking around King's Cross with my intestines hanging out!

'Audrey, please go back in. You're scaring me!'

I was terrified. I couldn't understand how we were both alive. I
thought I was done for. *Oh gosh, I'm going to have to go to hospital
and show them what I've done.* I've broken my stoma, plus I'll
never make it to Scott's party now. I'll have to call Radio 2 and let
them know. What if they don't have anyone else to cover? I *am*
the cover. I'm the person they call when someone is ill. I can't be
ill. I've ruined so many things today. What a mess. I had to try to
get my mutant Audrey back in. I had to confess . . .

Me: 'Kate, come here.'

Kate: 'Are you OK?'

Me: 'Don't kick off, but I think there's something wrong with
Audrey . . .'

Kate: 'What do you mean don't kick off?'

Me: 'Don't be scared, but I think she's broken . . .'

Kate enters the bathroom. Kate's soul leaves her body. Kate is
deceased. Kate doesn't speak. Kate is wondering WTF that big
mutant elephant trunk is hanging from my torso.

Me: 'I think I've prolapsed.'

I'll be honest, I'd done a little googling on my phone before
Kate had come in. I was just checking. I was checking I wasn't
already dead.

Kate: 'I'm calling an ambulance.'

Me: 'No!'

Kate: 'No?!'

Me: 'Yes. No. I can't miss Radio 2 tonight.'

Kate looked at me like I was an absolute muppet.

Kate: 'You are not going in to Radio 2.'

Me: 'I am. Google what to do.'

Kate googled, then helped me carry my intestine into the bedroom. I needed to lie down.

A quick disclaimer for the next part of the story: please do not try this at home. I am an idiot. I should have called for help straight away. After I refused an ambulance, Kate said that we should at least call Elaine, my stoma nurse. I didn't. I was scared we'd get done.

I was so angry with Audrey. She'd obviously been trying new tricks. She'd hulked out and got stuck. She reminded me of the time my brother got his head stuck through the bannisters on our stairs at home. My dad had to saw him out. That bannister has still not been replaced. It serves as a warning to all future curious children not to poke their heads in places they don't belong. Audrey's head was stuck in my bannister. I felt like sawing her off to teach her a lesson.

Kate: (*looking at her phone*) 'Have we got any sugar?'

Me: 'What?'

Kate: 'Have we got any sugar?'

Me: 'White or brown?'

Kate: 'It doesn't matter! Have we got any?'

Me: 'Yeah, I think so . . .'

Kate ran to the kitchen and returned with a bag of ice and a bag of sugar. She covered the bed with my puppy pads and asked me to lie on top. She then told me to pull my top up and my pants down.

By the way, all the time this is happening, Scott Mills is on Radio 1 having the final show of a lifetime and making the nation cry. It was nuts!

Kate: 'I think we can get her to go back in with ice or sugar.'

This sounded like the shittest spell ever.

Me: 'Icing sugar?'

Kate: 'No, ice OR sugar. We'll try the ice first.'

Kate then proceeded to put a bag of ice on my elephant trunk. It hurt like hell. I lay there for about five minutes. Kate lifted up the ice to see how it was going. Audrey had turned white, she looked dead! My intestine had gone from bright pink to lifeless white.

Kate: 'Shit. Please let me call an ambulance!'

Me: 'No!'

Kate: 'Let's try the sugar.'

With Scott Mills blaring and Audrey dying, Kate delicately sprinkled the sugar like she was dusting a cake.

Me: 'Just bloody pour it on!'

Kate went for it. She pretty much dumped 1kg of sugar onto my wet, icy torso. If somebody had walked in at that point, they would have thought we were proper wrong 'uns.

And that's when it happened – a miracle. As Scott Mills played 'We Don't Talk About Bruno', Audrey started to shrink. Slowly but surely, my insides stopped being so . . . outside. Bit by bit, my intestine disappeared, and after about 45 minutes, Hulk Audrey was no more. My elephant trunk was back to being a mere little carrot on the torso of my person.

I was amazed. I couldn't believe it. I don't know why or how it works, but it does.

Kate: 'You're going to be off your head on sugar now.'

I didn't care. I had a party to go to and a radio show to do. I sat up, ready to clean myself off, have a shower and get going again. Nope. Not so fast. It hurt. A LOT. I sadly had to miss Scott's party. To this day, I don't know if he knows why. But I do know that his last show was amazing. A super stoma-inducing show. Yep, Scott Mills I love you so much you make my stoma prolapse. Now that's a Valentine's card I'd like to write.

I did make it into Radio 2, believe it or not. I was still very sore and I had to sit down for the whole show, but I made it.

Now how does the song go?

Just a spoonful of sugar helps the stoma go down . . .

I should have ended the show with that one. Ha ha.

And those, my friends, were *Audrey's Greatest Hits*. Or *Now That's What I Call Audrey* coming to a record shop near you soon. Despite all the chaos, the uncertainty is a gift. It's a blessing. It reminds me once again of one of the great truths of life: you can't control what happens to you in life, but you can control how you react. It's been so good for me to have this constant reminder. Without it, I forget. I go back to my old habits. They're ingrained in me. I was the living dead for over 40 years. These changes won't come overnight, but I'm so happy I'm finally waking up. I'm getting my life back. I'm doing the work. I'm unclogging the sink hole, plunging with all my might, getting rid of the blockages. It's not pleasant seeing all my old junk coming to the surface – there are some fatbergs in my sewers, believe me – but it feels good to get my life moving again, letting go of the way I think things need to be, enjoying the movie of life without trying to rewrite the script. Don't get me wrong, I mess up every day. I'm rubbish at all this, but the key thing is I'm aware of it all now. Audrey is my constant reminder. I didn't *expect* to learn such a powerful life lesson from my small intestine (who now has a name and lives on the outside of my torso), but I *appreciate* her every single day. She's keeping me alive, in more ways than one.

NOTE TO SELF:
EXPECT NOTHING,
APPRECIATE EVERYTHING.

Sometimes The Going Gets A Little Tough
Finn

CHAPTER 9

'It seems our best ain't good enough.'

Sometimes the Going Gets a Little Tough

'You're cancer-free.'

It's the 19th of August 2022, and this is a moment I shall never forget; seconds I shall treasure forever, a breathtaking milestone I never knew I'd have the privilege of experiencing, a memory so stunning it still gives me butterflies. I never want it to leave me. It's in my soul. We'd travelled through the eye of the storm and out to the other side. Bobbing in our little boat, me, Kate and Audrey. We were now in uncharted territory with new lands to discover. We were lucky. We were free.

My body collapsed inwards as the words connected and knocked the emotion out of me. I didn't know it was in there; I didn't know I was holding on. Months of worry and fear rushed out of my body. I think I was so used to being in warrior mode and so focused on getting through chemo that I forgot this day might come. I forgot I might actually get some good news, that I might actually be OK. Oh, the irony – getting told I had cancer didn't knock me on my arse, getting told I was cancer-free did. Fancy that! It's the nicest sucker punch I've ever encountered. I might stay on the canvas for this one and enjoy the knockout.

I can finally relish the moment now, but at the time, my head was spinning. It was another sliding door moment. Another hospital room, another pair of chairs and me and Kate ready to face whatever was going to happen. Oh, and Audrey, of course. Our little trio. My team. My little family. We don't count our chickens anymore; we just stick them in a field and hope for the best.

As wonderful and amazing as hearing 'you're cancer-free' sounds, it comes with caveats. It comes with terms and conditions. It essentially means that there's no sign of cancer in your body *at the moment*. It's not been picked up on the tests and machines. Great news, I'll take it, but it doesn't mean it won't come back. So yes, I was cancer-free, but I was also now starting the next part of my journey. I'm currently on a monitoring programme where I'm regularly screened for cancer. The first two years after being treated for cancer is the period when it's most likely to reoccur. I'm currently in those two years as I'm writing this. Every scan I have done and the results that go with it are another chance for me to hear those words again. So far so good. Thankfully, I'm still 'cancer-free'; no cancer has reoccurred in my bowel and I'm still doing well with my recovery. The first big milestone will be if I make it to five years cancer-free. Imagine that. I pray for that day. It'll be amazing. My Auntie Ann recently celebrated ten years cancer-free – get in!

I have so many things to be grateful for, but I'm also very careful not to take this journey for granted. I guess that's what made it hard when I told people I was cancer-free. It should have been so special – and it *was* – but I also felt like I was lying somehow. I couldn't fully enjoy the moment with them. I felt bad. I knew I shouldn't have felt like this, but I didn't quite get to revel in the full feeling of it being over. I guess it'll never be over – cancer will always be that spectre peering just over my shoulder. The good news is I'm on to it now. I'm awake. I'm aware. The old 'me' thought I was cancer-free my whole life. The new me knows I'm lucky to be cancer-free every day that continues.

'Hello, I've Got Cancer'

Another thing it's good to brace yourself for is the strange reactions from *others* when you first tell them you have cancer. I decided to talk openly about my diagnosis because I felt very lucky to have a platform where I could share my experience and hopefully help others. So many people have helped me and Kate by sharing their stories online, on Instagram, on forums. We couldn't get enough of all the different authentic lived experiences. It made it much easier for us to know what could happen and to deal with what we were going through.

Being a bit more public meant I had to have some difficult conversations though. It's bad enough being told you have cancer, how do you then tell others, especially people not in your family? The 'Hello, I've got cancer' reaction spectrum is very varied: most people are how you'd expect, bloody lovely. They check in, let you know they're there if you need them and let you get on with it. Some people avoid you like the plague, while others act like they don't know it's happened (when you know they do) and just pretend it doesn't exist. Some will go the other way and pretty much ask you to move into their house so they can care for you and feed you Lucozade and grapes. It's fascinating and amazing, and no matter how people reacted, I think deep down I knew that, if I needed them, they'd be there. I felt very lucky, supported and loved. When the chips are down you realise there's more good than bad in this world. I promise. Humankind – there's nothing like it.

I guess the winner for the most bizarre reaction was from a former work colleague, someone I really like and a person I'd not seen since I'd been diagnosed. A lot of time had passed; I think it was about a year. I thought they'd be happy to see me. Here are the first words out of their mouth:

'So you're still with us? Not dead then?'

Yes, they actually said that. Kate says it to me from time to time to make us laugh. Why would someone say that?! (Note to self: it's OK to keep thoughts in your head. You don't have to say them out loud. Ha ha.) So humans can be kind and humans can be strange sometimes. Someone else I had to tell for work purposes pretty much said, 'OK' and put the phone down on me. But that was right at the start, so maybe I was a bit rubbish at the 'telling' bit then. It doesn't make things easier when, as a society, we don't talk about cancer enough and so we mainly only have what we see in the media to show us what it's like.

My whole perception and attitude towards cancer has changed. It used to be something I'd ignore or pretend wasn't happening. It used to be a monster to me. But cancer's actually a little bitch. It's pathetic. It's sneaky and snivelling. It's a sad internet troll hiding behind a screen, relying on us not revealing it. It's the man behind the curtain. Don't give it power. It relies on us having fear and not speaking about it. It relies on being the stuff of our nightmares. Well, it can do one. Speak its name! Drive it out! Let's all have each other's backs and be on guard together. Let's take our power back. Let's stare into the belly of the beast, stand tall and show it who it's messing with. And, as if by divine timing, the perfect opportunity for me and Audrey to do just that came along.

This next bit warmed my cockles and gave me a reason bigger than I could have imagined to stare into the face of cancer. Whitney wasn't joking when she said she believes the children are the future. They are. They might have just come to save us.

A Job for Audrey

This was seriously one of my highlights of 2022. Audrey, little Audrey, had been invited to a party. We'd been asked to take part in a Zoom session for the children's stoma support group they have at Great Ormond Street Hospital. It's an excellent idea and a safe space for the young patients to meet each other, make friends, share their experiences and encourage each other. I felt very privileged to be asked to be a part of it. Seeing those faces and hearing their stories connected with me in a way I hadn't anticipated. Those children built me up more than they could imagine. I felt so lucky that they would even begin to share their stories, their ups and downs, their struggles and triumphs with me. I was in awe of them. If I thought what I'd been through was challenging, it was nothing compared to these young souls. And there they were, still growing and making their way in the world the best they could.

Every child in the group has a stoma. For some, it may have been due to digestive conditions, while others had been through cancer like me. All had been through tougher times than most of us could imagine. But there they all were, smiling, happy, positive and willing to help me and let me in. As we went further into the session, I learned of all the extra pressures they had to deal with on top of what they were already going through: other children not understanding, the mean comments, the bullying, the wider world not being aware of their unique conditions. It felt like they spent a lot of their time trying to make do in order to fit in, hide away and manage their stomas in secret, away from their school friends. Some of their friends didn't even know they had one. I could totally understand why: they didn't want to have to deal with the judgement, the questions, the constant explaining why they might have to eat differently or wear different clothes.

It made me think of all the times I might have been insensitive or made someone feel uncomfortable. How ignorant of others had I been? I hoped I hadn't made anyone else feel odd. I hoped I'd not gone bumbling around life making others feel invisible. If I did, I am so sorry. This is another reason I'm so grateful to have a stoma. It's not just been life-saving; it's been life-changing. It's made me a better person for sure. It's also given me purpose: I want to do everything I can to make the world as understanding, mindful and accepting of ostomates as possible. Hundreds of thousands of people in the UK are ostomates, but many people don't know or aren't aware. I totally get it, me too, until recently. Plus, stomas and stoma bags are often not seen. They're under clothing. They're classed as a non-visible disability. That's why I want to do my best to represent this amazing community and help raise awareness and visibility. Diversity, inclusivity and representation matter.

I hope the wonderful children of the stoma support group know how much they inspired me that day. They are all little warriors, and it broke my heart that some of them felt that they might not be understood or accepted. It made me determined to show up for them in any way that I could. Straight after that call, I sent my nephew Oskar (Audrey's partner in crime) a Buttony Bear – a teddy bear with a stoma; how amazing is that? Oskar doesn't have a stoma, but his bear does and he loves him with all his heart. If he ever meets another bear or another baby with a stoma, he'll be super excited. He won't question it or make that person feel like they're different. He'll know they're a superhero and they're very brave. Just like his bear. Just like Audrey. Oskar, I love you. You make me so proud to be your auntie. My sister Lesley had Oskar a month after I 'had' Audrey. We used to swap new mum stories all the time, ha ha!

The stoma squad got me, Kate and Audrey pumped! I was already super proud of Audrey, but now I had a whole squad of stoma friends to show up for too. I wanted to do something to celebrate them. They gave me so much courage. A few days after this inspiring call, I was offered an amazing opportunity to represent the ostomate community. This time, I was approached by the producers of a brilliant TV show that I have watched and loved for years. They wanted to meet me and have a chat about potentially taking part in their next series. Now, I'm sure you've already gathered this, but I don't usually fare well on TV. I'm the *Big Brother* loser, and I was the first camp mate chucked out of the *I'm a Celebrity* jungle. It turns out I *wasn't* a celebrity and you *did* get me out of there. I'm shit and I know it! I much prefer sitting at home with a takeaway, *watching* television. The only time I can actually enjoy being on it is when I think it might help someone or when there's a reason to be there that's greater than my nerves.

The show in question has a big physical challenge involved. It's hard enough *without* a stoma, but I knew that if I could take it on with Audrey, it might help to change the representation of ostomates for the better. I also hoped it might help anyone dealing with cancer and give them a little bit of hope. I thought it might help me too. It would be a great challenge to not only help me physically but also mentally. Something to help my body and mind recover from what it had been through. Another great routine to keep me and Audrey off the streets. It was perfect.

My body was still battered from chemo. I'd finished in May 2022 and I was auditioning for this TV show in August, but I felt ready. I knew I'd give it my all. It had come at just the right time – I was turning a corner, getting my life back.

So, I met the producers of the show. I told them all about the stoma community and how much it would mean to me to be a part of the show. I can't even begin to tell you how much Kate and I talked about it and imagined how good it could be. I could finally be on TV and not be shit. Well, I hoped not. Audrey might have other ideas . . . but that was all part of the fun. I knew it would be a challenge.

Everything was set: I'd passed my medical, I'd got my contract and there were just a few loose ends to tie up before I started training. I was so excited to begin and to meet everyone – professionals at the top of their game, a whole team of passionate, brilliant people from different backgrounds and all walks of life. I couldn't wait to be around such greatness and fully immerse myself. I knew that, no matter what happened on the show, just being a small part of it was a huge win. Let the magic begin!

Kate read out a WhatsApp message she'd just received. It was for me. I'm not on WhatsApp. I know, I know – I just can't deal with it. I also don't really do DMs. One of my colleagues once said to me, 'Nothing good ever happens in the DMs,' and, from that day, I stopped reading them. It can get pretty wild in there. It's not for me, but thank you. To be honest, if I didn't need my phone for talking to my family, listening to music and keeping up with my Candy Crushing, I might not really use that either. Email is good for me. Kate once told me that she'd read somewhere that phones are supposed to be for our convenience, not everyone else's. Good advice, I think! When I was in hospital, I didn't use my phone at all apart from speaking to my family and taking photos of Audrey. No internet, no social media. It was bliss. If something disturbs your peace of mind, it's too high a price to pay. Don't ever feel obliged to be on call for others 24/7. Unless it's an emergency, it can wait. You matter, not your phone.

So, back to Kate's WhatsApp.

Kate: 'What does this mean?'

Me: 'What does *what* mean?'

Kate: (*reading*) '"Sorry to hear about the show. We're here for you if you need anything."'

I looked at Kate's phone. I read the message. I had no idea what it was on about. Kate tried to find out. After a few messages back and forth, we found out that I'd been chucked off the show. WTF?! How? Why? Was this a mistake?

It turned out that even though I'd already been told that I'd passed the medical, I'd failed a blood test. I had a very low iron count. What did that mean? Is it serious? Can I just nip to Wilko and get some iron tablets, or do I need a blood transfusion? Surely I could get help?

I called the doctor who worked on the show. He was so lovely to me, but it was such a hard phone call. I really believed that this experience would not only help me but it would help others too. Surely I could just get help for my low iron count and carry on. I was amazing at popping pills – I'd just had six months' practice on chemo. It was still a no. I felt helpless. The doctor said he knew that it must be hard for me to take, but he also believed that everything occurs for a reason and that something better could happen for me in the future. I was crushed, but I knew there was nothing I could do. I also knew deep down that he was right. As much as it hurt, I appreciated his time.

It seems so dramatic looking back, but it hurt so much. My thoughts went on a downward spiral. I felt like a failure. Maybe I wasn't getting better after all. I was lying to myself; I was delusional. I'd tried to focus on the good, do everything I could to stay positive, work towards regaining my health and reclaiming my body. I knew I wasn't perfect, but I was trying. And I wasn't good enough. I was beaten, and this was the sucker punch. It wasn't really that I wasn't going to be part of the TV show or that I now wouldn't be meeting new people, learning new skills and working towards a goal. It was the cancer. I felt like it had won. It had stopped me living my life how I wanted. This had meant more to me than getting *my* life back; I had hoped it would show others what's possible.

That's when it hit me – 'it' being the last year or so of my life; everything that had happened since my diagnosis. Guilt, shame, sadness, shock, unworthiness all piled on top of me. I was so 'in my feelings', I was under them – it was a real pity party for one. (We all need a little pity party from time to time, don't we?) My pity parties don't happen often, but when they do, boy do I party. My parties go on for days. I felt so rotten. So there we were – Auds and I – still in shock, still feeling a bit like they'd made a mistake, wondering what to do next. We got the morbs.

Got the morbs: a Victorian era slang phrase used to describe someone afflicted with temporary sadness or melancholy.

There was only one thing to do: activate my 'in my feelings' playlist, climb in the hurt locker and sit it out, wait for the storm to pass. Sometimes you have to pick your battles. It's weird – it's never the boulders in life that get me, it's always the pebbles. They seem to hurt me more. On the grand scale of things, this was just a small thing. I knew I'd get over it. I just didn't want to *have* to get over it. I was being a brat. I was just gutted. IT COULD HAVE BEEN SO GOOD! It's only bloody iron. I'll eat some spinach or something. The doctor was right though; my iron levels were dangerously low. Even my GP was like, *Bloody hell, you're seriously anaemic. Why hasn't this been picked up by the hospital?* I didn't know, but I thought it might be because they were spending all their time screening my blood for cancer. I don't think they gave two shits about iron.

So amor fati and all that. It was a blessing in disguise. This wasn't happening *to* me, it was happening *for* me . . . yada yada yada. I get it. When things go wrong it can be bloody annoying reading stuff like this. But it's true, so get ahead of the game. Save your memes for a rainy day. Do the work before you need it. That's a game changer in itself. Get ready when you're happy. It not only makes it easier to get started, but it actually makes you happier in the process. Change before you have to. Take on these ideas and principles when you're feeling good, so that when things go wrong or you're feeling bad, the antidote is already inside you – you just need to activate it. It's great practice. I love learning. I love finding new ways of thinking about things and I often save a lot of my positive thinking quotes when I'm already happy, when things are good and I don't need them. I think about my life, things I've overcome before, and I test them out. I hold on to the ones that work for me. I save them in my digital diary – my second brain. They're saved in my app under the hashtag 'note to self' so that when my bird brain starts screaming and kicking off because I've got low iron, I remember to chill the hell out and calm down. It doesn't stop the panic and the hurt immediately – we all need time to process feelings; we're only human – but I don't worry about negative feelings anymore. I know they're all part of the process.

Kate's helped me a lot with this. She's the total opposite to me. She's so beautiful, inside and out. It's like she's been conceived by the mind of Walt Disney. When she walks by an open window, birds and butterflies will fly out of the sky and lovingly sit on her shoulder. If they see me, they close the curtains and fly off . . .

Just being around Kate and seeing how she operates, seeing how she cares for herself, has shown me another way of being. She always leads with kindness. Kate makes me want to be a better person. I want to make better choices because of her: not to be so impulsive; stop fighting fire with fire. She's helped me to chill out and let go, to sit back and enjoy life. I still struggle with a lot of things, but that's the beauty of it all – I'm learning how to be better and I'm loving it. I'm starting to be more aware of my flaws and I'm enjoying making changes. I'm getting stronger by feeling my feelings, not ignoring them or holding on to them; I'm allowing the feelings to flow right through me.

It's healthy to feel. Let the feelings go: run them out, walk them out – do what works for you. Get physical, and before you know it, your body starts to release the hurt, the frustration and the pain. I always find that when I move my body, I move forward in my life. Be the sitting duck as long as you need to, but then get moving again. It's much harder for the morbs to hit a moving target.

I still don't know why my iron count is low. It could be due to my stoma or it could be the damage the chemo has done to my blood (chemo is very good at destroying red blood cells). It could also be that I'm genetically predisposed to having a low iron count. We don't know. I now have regular blood tests for my iron levels and I'm receiving treatment for it, which is great. A brown pill a day keeps the anaemia away – for now. I think they'll properly sort it out once I have my stoma reversal (if that's possible, at the moment it's not).

I had had my moment, my wobble, the toys had come out of my pram, but it was a beautiful lesson. Looking back, I'm super grateful for this time in my life. It was only a little blip in the grand scheme of things; it just felt bigger to me because that's where I'd placed all my focus. I needed to learn to zoom out and get perspective.

'Be thankful for what you have; you'll end up having more. If you concentrate on what you don't have, you will never, ever have enough.'
– Oprah Winfrey

Life was good: I'd managed to finish chemo; I was 'cancer-free'; I had my family; I had Kate; I had my little Audrey; I got to meet the incredible and inspirational children of Great Ormond Street . . . I just didn't get to go on a TV show. What a great 'problem' to have. In fact, it wasn't a problem at all. It was a privilege. I had the privilege of auditioning for a TV show and I just didn't make the cut. No harm done. Nobody died. I was alive! I needed to refocus and count my blessings. Without the TV show, I might not have known about my low iron count. It could have been very dangerous. I got the help I needed. I had so much to be thankful for.

NOTE TO SELF:
THERE ARE NO LOSSES IN LIFE, ONLY WINS AND LESSONS.

Have Yourself a Merry Little Christmas
Judy Garland

CHAPTER 10

'Next year all our troubles
'Will be out of sight.'

Have Yourself a Merry Little Christmas

It's a wonderful life! Welcome to Christmas Day 2022. Kate is about to microwave a chicken korma meal that she got from the local garage for lunch. She should be wearing her fancy, sparkly dress, but instead she's got my Primark trackie on. I'm wearing my usual black get-up, though I also have more fancy clothes that I should be wearing (not a sparkly dress though). Despite this, the way the day unfolded was a true Christmas miracle. It was proof of the strength of the human spirit and the kindness of others. It was the best Christmas present I've ever received – the people and the moments that helped to save my mum; the very proof that there are angels and heroes all around us.

It all began with me trawling the streets at 6am. I was up trying to find a shop that was open, and I was panicking. What shops would be open on Christmas Day – and at this time? I needed unforeseen supplies. I needed to find something to help soothe my mum. I drove around looking for signs of life. I'd gone about five miles down the road when I saw my northern star. I felt like the wise men trying to find baby Jesus. I eagerly followed my beacon of hope – the Spar sign gleaming under the dark Preston sky. Alas, would they let me in? I parked up and walked nervously across the deserted forecourt. I had everything crossed and hoped they could help me. It was one of those garage-cum-shop-cum-mini-mart thingies. It looked epic and I wanted in! As I approached, the large, electric stable door opened. I was allowed entry. I could have cried with happiness. I hunted for some supplies that I thought might help my mum. I didn't know what to buy, so I did the best I could. I bought her protein shakes and Sudocrem. (What? I had to improvise.) I did my Spar supermarket sweep and got back in the car ready to set off back to Kate who was safely tucked up in bed. I didn't want to disturb her peace. I wanted her to get some sleep. It had been a bumpy 48 hours already. I couldn't sleep that morning worrying about my mum. It was only a few days before that I'd heard about her accident. It was all so new to me so I hadn't really had time to process it. I just prayed we'd get her the help she needed and we'd do what we could in the meantime.

I sat in the car and started it up, ready to set back off. Kelly Clarkson's version of 'Have Yourself a Merry Little Christmas' started playing on the radio. I was so happy at that moment, I could have cried – the perfect song playing the perfect message at the perfect time.

So that was my first gift on Christmas morning: fate asking Kelly Clarkson to sing a Judy Garland classic to me, letting me know everything would be all right. All delivered through the prism of Smooth FM . . . and yes, I listen to Smooth. I rarely used to listen to the actual radio station I worked for. I've always done this. I get to learn from other presenters, and it stops me being too 'in the bubble', plus I get to be a listener again . . . and Smooth FM is banging! 'It's a relaxing mix with the best music' don't you know? It has fabulous presenters too; I love them all – Jenni, Kate, Tina aka Hobbo . . . and Angie. Oh Angie Greaves, you are a goddess. I cannot begin to tell you how much I love Angie on Smooth. She's the Rolls-Royce of radio. She's steered me through some tough times I tell you. She makes me and Kate so happy. She makes the art of radio sound so simple, but it's not – that's years of Angie honing her craft. She's one of the greats.

As I've touched on, radio has always been the one for me – especially BBC Radio 1. It's only recently that I've understood why. It was my mum's station of choice. It was always on in our house, filling the air with sweet music and flooding our space with good vibes. BBC Radio 1 = Preset 1 in our car too. Mum always used to tell me about the time when the Radio 1 Roadshow came to Southport: Gary Davies in his short shorts (I think she had a soft spot for him) and thousands of people on Southport Promenade, having the time of their lives. It was one of her best memories from when she was younger. Her face used to light up when she'd tell me about it. It made me so happy to see her so happy. I've come to realise, after many years of thinking it was MY dream, that my mum is a huge part of the reason I wanted to be on the radio. In fact, she *is* the reason. I wanted to make her happy. I wanted to make her proud. I wanted to be part of that roadshow for her. I hope I did that for you, Mum.

My mum lost her dad when she was 13. Within three years, by the age of sixteen, she'd lost her mum too, and then she had me – a baby with a baby. She kept that child clothed, fed, protected and with a roof over its head. My mum achieved more in those three years than I ever have or ever could. I've always known her greatness. I think I've always wanted to give her something that the outside world would recognise as 'great' too. Her dreams became my dreams. Now I think about it, I'm merely her tribute act. She's my hero; I'm her shadow.

Mum was the first person in our family to have records. She had these two little, perfectly square record boxes, one black, one red, full of pristine 7-inch records with gold locks on the front to keep them safe. I was in love with them. I'd sit and go through them for hours. I treated them like precious antiques – picking up each record gently and handling them with the utmost care, looking at the beautiful artwork on the front, reading the covers and trying to hear the wonderful music locked inside. We didn't have a record player, so all I could do was imagine. Sometimes I'd be able to match the title of her records to songs on the radio. One of my favourites was Squeeze's 'Cool For Cats'. Not only did I love hearing my mum singing along to it whenever it played, but I'd also think of the gorgeous 7-inch record she possessed. It was made of baby pink vinyl. It was stunning – a magical unicorn in her record box of tricks, a real one-off. I adored it! I used to pretend it was made of strawberry milkshake. It was so beautiful I wanted to eat it.

So I guess I've worked it out: my mum was actually the first DJ to save my life.

My first record was thanks to my mum. She got it free with my first pair of shoes. Clarks shoes, proper shoes – Mum-approved shoes! She loved the bright red patent leather sandals she got for me that day. She'd saved all her money for those little clodhoppers. I think she was super proud. It made her so happy every time I wore them. I, on the other hand, loved the sleek black shiny vinyl that came with them. A gift for each of us: Mum got me to wear ruby-red Dorothy shoes; I got to have a record by Adam and the Ants – the fabulous 'Prince Charming'. Yes please, this was the best day ever! Mum said I used to run over to the TV whenever Adam Ant was on it. I'd catch a glimpse of his punky, new romantic frame and know it was time – time to whip out my sweet moves, the whole 'Prince Charming' dance routine executed with perfect co-ordination. It was automatic. I was in a trance. I was hooked. From what I can gather now, the 'Prince Charming' 'routine' is similar to 'flexing the X' like they do on *The X Factor* . . . over and over until the song finishes. Yep, that's the extent of my dance skills, but to three-year-old me, I was living! I was obsessed with Adam Ant. I think my mum was too. He was a vision in make-up who looked like a super cool pirate and a dandy all at the same time. Tall, dark and handsome with bright blue eyes, Mum well fancied him.

My mum has a lot to answer for. If Jackie loved it, then I instantly did too. I even ended up going to a fancy posh big school because of her – the prestigious Merchant Taylors' School for Girls. We'd see the pupils of the school from time to time as we ricocheted and pinged from council house to council house around the North West. Mum would say, 'You'll go to that school one day.' She claims I was the one who always wanted to go, but, to be honest, I don't remember it like that. I think I just assumed I'd be going because my mum said I would, and all I ever wanted to do was please her. I'd look at the girls in their fabulous, pristine, navy-blue uniforms, straw hats and posh blazers and imagine what their school would look like. *I bet it looks like the Houses of Parliament; I bet they play hockey and lacrosse* (they do).

On paper, there was no way a girl like me should be going to that school. We couldn't afford it and you needed to pass an entrance exam to even be considered for a place. Not the best start for me. Thanks to moving around so much, I'd missed large parts of the curriculum, especially English. I'd gone from being quite a good reader in primary school to not even being able to write proper sentences in junior school. Each school I'd attended was different, so with each new school tie around my neck, I'd often have to start my learning all over again and try my best to keep pace with the other children. I spent a lot of time catching up instead of learning new stuff. My mum could have gone to my posh high school in a heartbeat. She'd passed her 11+ exam with ease and could have gone to any independent or grammar school in the land. She's so clever; she has a natural brilliance. Her brain is so sharp, and, along with Kate, she's easily one of the most naturally gifted people I know. And with my mum, there were also no excuses; when she knew what she wanted to do, she set about it in her own way. She had no one to ask for help so she helped me herself.

My mum became my tutor. I remember her taking me to WHSmith to get an exercise book. *This is strange*, I thought, *Mum's actually buying me a book* (we didn't do books in our house – only comics. We were allowed *The Beano* and *The Dandy* because my dad liked them). Looking back, it must have been a revision guide designed to help children prepare for entrance exams. The only problem was, at that point, I wasn't revising anything – I was still learning. I was seeing most of this stuff for the first time. *Ah, so that's a verb? That's a noun? And you need one of each to make a sentence? Cool. Where do these adjective things go then?* It was a weird time in my life, but it was wonderful. My mum wasn't like one of those TV mums who did cuddles and quality time or things like reading to us at bedtime. That all sounds super lovely and a very nice idea, but with three kids by that point, no money and juggling benefits and jobs, she didn't have bloody time. She always seemed to have mountains of washing, mouths to feed, bills to pay, things to do, but, to her credit, she made sure that she gave me as much of her time as she could, and she'd help me at the end of each exercise. I'd sit and work alone through each one, trying my best. Mum would then mark my work and help me to see where I'd gone wrong. She's amazing – essentially a girl who'd not really been in school herself and left way before her exams, teaching another girl who'd missed most of her formative years of junior school. All of this not only helped me to catch up, but to be of a standard where I could pass the entrance exam to 'mini Eton'. I don't know how she did it, but from that wobbly makeshift table in our council house, with its ripped wallpapered rooms and serious lack of space, furniture and carpets, I passed the exam and got myself a golden ticket to the school that would change my life. All thanks to my mum – my beautiful, brilliant, gold-hoop-earring-wearing hero. I got a full scholarship which was paid for by the government. They took care of everything – we couldn't afford any of it . . . not the uniform, nor the bus pass, my train pass, or the thousands of pounds in fees for each term.

My school was 15 miles away. I'd have to get up at 6.30am each day, get a bus to Southport train station, then a train to Crosby, followed by a 30-minute walk to school, and then I was ready for the day, ready to start. Those years were some of the best of my life; I treasure them. I loved that school with all my heart. I also knew how lucky I was to be there. I wished the other kids from our estate could have joined me. I had nothing compared to the girls I went to school with, but they never made me feel poorer for it, or any different. I was treated as an equal and welcomed with open arms. Thanks to that school, I got another snapshot of how incredible life could be, how the other half lived. And it was all because of my mum. All thanks to her self-less love. She started small so I could dream big.

But I guess life doesn't always care for potential or intelligence or brilliance. There are so many bright and special souls, all around us, hidden by fate and bound by circumstance. My mum had no one to encourage her, believe in her and help her dreams come true. Instead she took all that love and support she should have had and gave it to us, her children – all six of us. What a woman. Records, red shoes, routines and radio. All for you, Mum.

Radio Head

I used to love doing early breakfast on Radio 1, especially at Christmastime – it is even more special then. I loved hearing the Christmas music and the messages that would come in from the listeners, especially the ones from the good people of the UK – those who keep the country moving while everyone else is sleeping. The legendary early-morning crew: the emergency services, the farmers, the lorry drivers, the overnight workers, the cleaners, the flight attendants, the parents up early caring for their children, people travelling home after being away from their loved ones.

Radio 1 is such a special club that I felt very lucky to have been a part of. When I first got the job, Greg James sent me a message to say congratulations and that I was about to experience the most magical time of the day. He wasn't wrong. There's nothing like it. It was one of the reasons I was so excited when I was asked to do the early breakfast show on Radio 2 in the week before Christmas – the former home of the incredible, formidable force that is Vanessa Feltz. What an absolute powerhouse. She used to present early breakfast on Radio 2 and then nip across the road to do the breakfast show on BBC London. Sometimes she'd then whip on a helmet, jump on the back of a motorbike and get ferried to the *This Morning* studios to present bits on there. What a unit. I'll have some of what she's drinking. Give me the custard! (If you don't know the custard story, please google it. I really hope it's true. If so, she's an even bigger legend than I thought.)

I really felt like I'd arrived. Radio 2 is classy and I needed to up my game. Kate made me wear my nice clothes for the week. It's a different energy. Different gravy. They've got a grand piano just casually lying around by the kitchen. There's a coffee machine. They don't do granules, darling, they do espresso and cappuccino. They're even allowed to have food and drink in their studios! What is this life? They also have proper Christmas decorations. If Radio 1 are Waitrose, then Radio 2 are Fortnum & Mason. They don't mess about. Radio 1 doesn't really bother with decor. They might put a bit of tinsel on a mic stand, but Radio 2? Radio 2 deck the halls with balls of holly. They go to town.

The listeners of Radio 2 also know the correct lyrics of that song I've just mentioned. It's not 'balls of holly', is it? I can't remember what it's supposed to be, but I do remember that they had a lot of fun correcting me. It was the week of dreams. I loved every second.

I was on from 4am to 6.30am, just before Zoe Ball took over with her team to wake up the nation. Zoe is absolutely how you'd expect BTW. Believe the hype. She is as lovely and as gorgeous as she is tall. She lights up the room, star quality in abundance. The passion just pours out of her. I managed to watch her do a few of her links. It was effortless. Her words come from the heart; she means it, pouring positivity into the microphone and out into the world. What a way for her listeners to wake up. Zoe and her team really made me feel part of the family – she even got me a Christmas card and a little present at the end of the week. How thoughtful and kind is that? A beautifully packaged sweet treat just for me, and one of my favourites too: fudge. Ooof . . . I couldn't wait to take it home to show everyone. I pretty much spent all Christmas saying, *Do you want to try some of this fudge? It's Zoe Ball fudge.* And they did. It was gone within minutes. So yes, proper good eggs all round at Radio 2.

I had the week of my life, surrounded by world-class production teams and presenters and playing copious amounts of Christmas music, soundtracking people actually driving home for Christmas. The listeners were so funny too. They cracked me up all week. Here are just a few of the things we talked about:

We pondered *when you hear Chris Rea singing 'Driving Home for Christmas', what car do you imagine him driving in?* A lot of people imagined him in a Rover or a white Vauxhall Cavalier. For me, it was always a white Ford Capri. Kate always imagines him driving a 'boxy, family-sized car with wood panelling that smells of cigs'. She also thinks he'll have a pine-scented Magic Tree air freshener, 'just because it's Christmas'. Ha ha. Kate, ever the actress, loves a good backstory.

There was more vitriol for my favourite Christmas song of all time, Wizzard's 'I Wish It Could Be Christmas Everyday'. That poor song. Poor Roy Wood.

Producer Nam: 'Those lyrics don't make sense – the snowman can't bring the snow, he IS the snow! It's stupid.'

She's got a point to be fair.

Then Paul McCartney's 'Wonderful Christmastime'. How could anyone have a go at this? Well, this one needs to be listened to to be appreciated. It's about one minute 30 into the song. Have a listen to the children singing.

Radio 2 Listeners: 'They've practised all year long to sing "ding dong" like that?! They're rubbish!'

I'm so glad I had the privilege of experiencing Radio 2 at Christmastime. It was so much fun from start to finish. I laughed so much sometimes that my tummy hurt.

My final show on Radio 2 was on Friday the 23rd of December, my sister's birthday. It's my yearly cue to pack up the car with Kate and little Audrey and head home to see our families. We love driving home for Christmas – Queen Angie Greaves helping to guide us home. It would be a little different this time. My sister had called me on the Sunday before I started the week on Radio 2 to say that Mum had hurt herself – she'd had a fall.

'A fall? Is she OK?'

Loren said she thought she'd be all right, but she'd hurt herself quite a bit and it was sore for her to sit down. I spoke to my mum. She seemed OK, but I felt like there was more happening than she was letting on. It's a nightmare trying to get the truth out of those two sometimes. Loren's condition makes it very hard for her to communicate and express herself. It also makes my mum not really see a fall or her injuries as severe, so she just dealt with that the way she deals with everything: she just got on with it.

All I knew at that point was that she was in some discomfort. I didn't worry too much, though, because my mum has carers who visit her and help her day to day. They're brilliant with her. They'd be there to help out at mealtimes, mornings to get dressed, night-time to help her get back into bed and anything else she needed. I knew she was being checked regularly and I figured surely somebody would have told me if it was really serious. I called my mum and asked her if I could do anything to help, but she said no. I suggested I get her a pressure cushion to help her body while she was sitting down and then maybe I could do more once I was back in Southport. I ordered some cushions for her and hoped they'd help in the meantime until I could be there in person to do more. Thank you to all the delivery services for keeping people connected and delivering those smiles at Christmastime. You helped my mum more than you could imagine.

I checked in with Mum on the phone each day. She seemed OK, but as the week progressed, I was starting to get worried. I felt like there was more to it. I just had to keep a lid on my emotions, try my best on Radio 2 and get home as soon as I could. Towards the end of the week, I spoke to my dad. He'd called to say I might not be able to take my mum out of the house for the Christmas meal I'd planned for us at a local restaurant. He also explained that he'd cancelled her carers over Christmas so they could have a break. I totally understand why he did this; it was a lovely gesture for the brilliant people who'd been caring for Mum all year round, but unfortunately he'd cancelled them before her fall, so it meant that, from Christmas Day, she wouldn't have anyone other than us. I just wanted to get home as soon as possible.

However, Kate and I have learned to pick our battles over the years when taking on the M1 and M6. As much as we appreciate them and as vital as they are, they can be cruel mistresses. We knew they'd both be rammed on a Friday and we wouldn't be getting home anytime soon. We also knew I'd be overtired and emotional due to being up at 2am to do Early Breakfast, so it was best to stay in London, rest up and travel home on Christmas Eve. We imagined most people would have travelled to their families on the Friday, so hopefully Saturday would be an easier journey. I couldn't rest or sleep or stop worrying about my mum – and Audrey went into overdrive.

It was Christmas Eve and time for our road trip. Audrey had been fidgeting all morning. I think me worrying about Mum gave her superpowers. Her stoma bag had no chance – it lasted until just past Birmingham. I could feel the bag coming off, so we decided to cut our losses, deal with the little demon in my pants and pull into the M6 services. We thought it best to change Audrey's bag in the car. I didn't have time to get to the toilet, it was too late and she was already hanging out. We parked up, positioning ourselves far away from all the other cars, over to a discreet section that was very quiet with no vehicles. Kate ran to the boot to get my change bag and I put the car seat down so I could lean back, stem the flow of Audrey's output and get a better sense of the damage. So seat back, pants down, T-shirt up and tucked under my bra. That's the very moment a family of four decided to come and park right by us and start eating bloody sandwiches. They were looking over to see what we were doing. I mean, what's suspicious about me lying back with my torso exposed and Kate bending over me? Totally normal. NOT! The dad even got out of the car and started walking their dog so he could get a better look. So essentially Kate and I took Audrey dogging on Christmas Eve and it wasn't even our fault.

Bag changed, M6 Toll paid and back on the road, off to see my mum. And can you believe it, when I got there she complained about one of the cushions I'd got for her! She's so funny. See what I have to put up with?

The reason she'd complained about the cushion is because it was hurting her bottom.

'Can I see, Mum?'

Kate and I lifted her up from her chair. She wasn't just sore from the fall; she was bleeding. She'd been sitting in a pool of her own blood. Tears flooded to my eyes. I had to try to act calm so as not to worry her. I think a combination of Mum just getting on with it, not really telling everyone how bad it was and her sitting on her sores all day meant she was bleeding constantly from her wounds. It took me ages to find out what had actually happened – it was like some messed-up jigsaw that I had to piece together. My mum's condition is so unique that, to be fair, even the hospital doesn't always know what to do. Everyone tries their best. There are so few people with the condition that it manifests differently in every person. My mum is totally different to my sister, for example. They're also at different points in their lives, so they both have different needs, struggles and dangers. But don't get it wrong, Ataxia – you might have transformed my mum physically, you may have changed her visually beyond all recognition, but her spirit remains. She is still just as fabulous as she ever was.

It turns out that my mum had tried to get herself out of bed during the night (she has a commode next to her so she can get herself to a toilet unaided). Unfortunately, this time she'd fallen and landed on the wooden floor. She couldn't get herself up because of her condition. It was also very cold – Merseyside December cold! – so she'd been out of bed on a freezing, hard, wooden floor. She couldn't call for help because her speech is affected and the only other person in the house at the time was my sister Loren, who has the same condition and accessibility needs. Mum got so cold that her body started to shake uncontrollably. The tremors ended up causing so much friction against the wooden floor that it took the skin off her body – my mum's beautiful dark skin torn to pieces, exposing the delicate pink skin underneath. She'd been found by a carer and my dad the following morning. The carers had done their best and dressed her wounds, but since then, things had taken a turn for the worse. Blood was now pouring out of her sores. It was horrific.

We called 111 immediately. They said we could take her to A&E, but to expect a long wait because it was Christmas. We couldn't really risk that. If we took her to hospital she would have needed to sit in her wheelchair and we knew her body wouldn't have been able to take it. It would have been an agonising wait. I asked Mum if I could put her in bed to take the pressure off her sores, but she said she didn't want me to. The other cushion I got her, the one she liked, would be enough. I nodded. I wanted to do more, but I also wanted to respect her wishes. I felt helpless. I wanted to get the hospital to come and get her. I wanted them to save her. But it was Christmas – there was nothing we could do.

An action plan was put into place. It would be a DIY Christmas dinner tomorrow. Kate and I would be waitresses and Mum and Loren would dine in the comfort of their own home. The food for them both would be lovingly prepared by my dad and brothers and sisters – a total family affair, just what Christmas is all about.

So here we are, Christmas Day lunch. Kate is in the kitchen microwaving our festive chicken kormas (this time from another Spar garage of dreams in Southport – see, angels everywhere). Muffin the dog is dining with us also. He eagerly awaits Loren throwing some food his way. Good luck, Muffin – I had a taste (sans cutlery, sans gravy) and it was truly one of the best Christmas meals I've ever had the privilege of eating. I ate most of it with my hands too.

Mum dined from the comfort of her recliner chair, complete with pressure pad cushion, a nice layer of Sudocrem to help soothe her sores, and me on the knife and fork to help cut up her food to make it manageable to eat. Now That's What I Call Christmas.

Christmas Day turned into Boxing Day and we got through it as a family. We just helped Mum as much as we could until normal 'Chrimbo limbo' business resumed. Together we made it to Tuesday the 27th of December, my brother Lloyd's birthday, and the day the carers returned. What a great present for Lloyd and for us all. It was a great day!

Note to self: don't put Sudocrem on open sores. I got told off by Mum's carers when they came back. I apologised and promised not to do it again (I did do it a few more times, but it was only because my mum asked. She was so sore and it seemed to help her. I'd rather get told off by the carers than by my mum to be fair. She's still got life in those lungs – I'm still scared of her!).

Kate and I were there each day to help take care of her and do what we could. I also managed to speak to the emergency adult services at the council over Christmas. Again, another example of how much good is in the world. The lady I spoke to was working from home and volunteering. She wasn't even getting paid and yet here she was making sure my mum got the help she needed. She was so amazing that, by Friday the 30th of December, less than a week after Christmas Eve, my mum had been placed in a nursing home and was getting the emergency care she needed from brilliant nurses who could help her. They estimated that she needed around six weeks of intense medical care to help get her back on track.

I don't know how Mum did it. She's got amazing strength and determination. There were so many times when we didn't think she'd pull through. Her weight kept dropping dangerously low and it took her body a long time to heal. I think she spent the first month or so just trying to survive. It affected her physically and mentally – she kept feeling like she was going to fall out of bed. She was so scared and it was heartbreaking. Ataxia is such a cruel condition. It's slowly shutting her body down around her, stealing her speech and clouding her memories, attempting to erase the things that make her her.

I don't want to speak on my mum's behalf, and I definitely wish she'd never had to experience any of this, but this to me is another example of something good coming out of something so harrowing. Being at the nursing home has been a blessing in disguise. She's still in her beloved Southport and all of the nurses at the home are exceptional at what they do – they are just wonderful. Her nurses are always in her room, caring for her or just chatting. They are not only meeting her medical needs but also giving her companionship. It's just beautiful. She's absolutely blooming. She was only supposed to go there for a few weeks to help her recover, but she now loves it there so much she doesn't want to go back home!

We've put an Alexa Echo Show in Mum's room, just by her bed. It has a feature on it that allows me to 'drop in' on her anytime and speak to her. My mum can't use a phone so I never really used to be able to contact her unless I was back in Southport or there was somebody with her who could help her. I can now video call her anytime and she doesn't have to pick up. I did it three times a day when she was first admitted. My brothers and sisters get to see her more. My sister Lesley has been wonderful and takes little Oskar to see her in person all the time. Mum loves it.

Kate and I 'drop in' every day now, usually just after she's had her dinner, with our daily quiz. She loves the quiz! It keeps her mind sharp and helps her remember all the things that have happened over her life. We tailor the questions to anything she might know. Her mind had started to deteriorate after her fall, and her condition also affects her cognitive function, but her mind is getting stronger every day. She remembers more than I do. And music – she loves music. Quite often her nurses will play music on her Alexa when they're in her room. It lights her up. They play her all sorts, but seem to particularly love eighties music, power ballads and Malaysian hip-hop. I asked Mum about it – she says the nurse who likes the hip-hop dances when he's with her. Ha ha.

I've started preparing playlists for her now, so when I'm with her, we'll play her music and get her to guess the song. She is so fast! You can see her memories flooding back in real time. It's so moving to see. It's like her body bursts into life as soon as she recognises a song. Ataxia doesn't stand a chance when her music is on. Her little feet will be tapping away and she'll be singing along to her heart's content. It's wonderful to witness. I've even taken my controller and taught her to DJ. The buttons on it are big and we help her to press them. I've taught her to use the crossfader too. She's a better DJ than me – LOL.

Kate and I get to see Mum much more in person since I've left my radio show. I made the decision to leave Radio 1 a few months after her fall. I got into it because of my mum, and it was only fitting that I stepped away when she needed me the most. I had the best time in radio – it was a dream come true. I had the privilege and the absolute pleasure of meeting people and experiencing things beyond my wildest dreams. I first stepped into a radio studio when I was 18. I made it until the age of 44 before I quietly snuck back out again. What a ride. What a special time. But I've had my time. It's now someone else's. My mum's fall and everything she's been through is a reminder of where I want to be – where I want to spend my time. Every day I get to be with her is an absolute blessing.

'I want my time with you.'
– Tracey Emin

I am so grateful to everyone who got us through that Christmas week. I truly believe you helped save my mum. I don't think she'd be here without you. A fall like that would be bad enough for anyone, but for a lady like my mum, who'd lost so much weight so quickly, with a condition like Ataxia, it was a miracle she got through it. And, once again, a great lesson for me. My mum has become one of my greatest teachers. She's still not back to the way she was before her fall, but considering what she's been through, her recovery has been incredible. What a champion. Her unstoppable spirit defies her condition and the body she now resides in. She embodies everything this book is about.

NOTE TO SELF:
IT'S NOT HOW MANY TIMES YOU FALL, IT'S HOW MANY TIMES YOU GET BACK UP.

Believe
Ministers de la Funk feat. Julie McKnight

CHAPTER 11

'If you believe,
You'll find a way.'

Believe

Well, here we are, my friends. Everything up to this point has led to the best stupidest idea I've ever had: attempting to run a marathon less than 18 months after life-changing surgery to remove a cancerous tumour from my body. Oh, and a stoma thrown in for good measure.

Yeah sure, great idea.

Idiot.

I don't know what I was thinking, but I'm glad I did. It turned out to be quite the adventure.

Over Christmas and the early weeks of 2023, I had a lot of time to think. Everything that had happened with my mum was still uppermost in my mind. I wasn't really thinking about what lay ahead for me and I didn't have any big plans. I was just taking it day by day. I definitely wasn't thinking about doing a new challenge. And besides, I had a new job – I was Mum's quiz show host! She was hooked on three quizzes a day at one point – we're now down to one round a day, thank goodness.

In the midst of my quiz master prep, I got a call from my friend Beth. Beth works with Nissan on their Possibilities Project. Not only do I love the name of this initiative, I also love everything it stands for: 'Zero emissions, zero inequalities. Helping to create more opportunities for people from underrepresented communities.' I'm very proud to be a diversity and inclusion ambassador for Nissan and, as part of my role, I get to represent and champion the wonderful LGBTQ+ community, supporting their running partnerships with events like the Great Run Series and the London Marathon. Nissan are one of the sponsors of the fabulous 'Rainbow Row' – a fully inclusive cheer zone along the London Marathon route, a larger-than-life celebration of the LGBTQ+ community, their families and allies. Rainbow Row feels like a mini pride parade and it's a safe space for all. It even comes complete with a DJ booth. At the last two marathons, I actually got to DJ on decks powered by one of Nissan's electric cars for all the runners and their supporters. I was in heaven. It was super cool.

2023 would see the London Marathon move back to its spiritual home of the month of April. (For the previous three years it had been held in October due to the Covid-19 pandemic.) Nissan had some places in the marathon and Beth asked if I knew anyone who might be interested in taking part. I said I'd mull it over and get back to her if I thought of someone. I was excited for whoever it would be. Getting a place in the London Marathon is huge and I knew whoever got that place would be very lucky. The demand for London Marathon ballot places is always oversubscribed, so you're very lucky if you get one. I guess it's like Glastonbury for runners.

It had been a long time since I'd been in the sort of shape where I could run a marathon. 2018 was the last time I'd taken part as a runner. I'd managed to complete two marathons before in my lifetime – that was more than good enough for me. Over the last year or so, my running had turned into jogging. Then my jogging turned into walking. Walking was my new thing. You can wear what you want to do it and, to me, as long as you're moving your body, you're moving forward in your life. That's my motto. Just do what you can, with what you have, exactly where you are. That's all you can do, isn't it? Your personal best. Walking was where my physical ability was and I was happy with it. I thought my marathon-running days were over.

It didn't stop me reminiscing though. Training for those marathons years before completely changed me, both physically and mentally. I absolutely went from couch to marathon – a huge transformation. It wasn't just about the running; I realised it was also about who I became in the process and all the valuable lessons I learned along the way – lessons that would help prepare me for the twists and turns of life, including that cancer curveball. Thank God I found running when I did, but it didn't come naturally to me at first.

I was first asked to take part in the London Marathon after *Big Brother*, way back in 2002. I said yes, but in my heart I didn't believe I could do it. So, in the end, I made my excuses and I didn't even try. I remember seeing Jade Goody attempt it a couple of years later. I can't remember what happened, but I don't think she finished, and the papers had a field day. I remember reading about her and thinking, *At least she tried*. I was the failure. I didn't even attempt it. At least she had the guts to give it a go. I admired her for that.

My sister Lois was the one who really lit a fire under my arse. In 2016 she signed up for the Southport Race for Life, a 5K for our Auntie Ann (my dad's sister, who is amazing and deserves a whole book of her own). Within the space of two years, my Auntie Ann lost our Uncle Phil to cancer and then had to go through it herself – without her husband. Lois wanted to do something in tribute to Auntie Ann and Uncle Phil and give back to the organisations that'd helped them. I remember sponsoring her, but I then forgot about it. Lois wasn't a runner and I didn't really know what a 5K was at that time. Was it far? Would she do it with friends? Would she do it at all? I mean, I was no one to talk – I was always saying I'd do stuff and then not doing it. I later found out that a 5K is 3.1 miles. Wow! Lois not only completed the race but also ran every step of the way with no training – just grit, determination and a reason to run in her heart. And she did it all on her own. Nobody was there to support her; no one was there to cheer her on; she just turned up on the day and went for it. When I saw the photo she posted afterwards, I couldn't believe it. My little sister was a hero, and there I was, still in bed. It still gives me goosebumps seeing that photo and knowing what it took for Lois to do that. Look what belief can do.

On Loose Women
– six weeks to go
until my scan to see
if I'm cancer-free.

Good Morning Britain.

In the ITV green room!

Taking my first dose of chemo.

Some side effects of chemo.

Jumping for joy - I am cancer-free!

Audrey's first holiday.

My nephew, Oskar, with his Buttony Bear.

Audrey's prolapse . . . Sugar to the rescue!

Training for the London Marathon.

My training gear.

Lois
544

RACE FOR LIFE FOR
my Auntie Ann

My sister Lois' race number, the photo that inspired me to run.

Couch to marathon for me in 2017. Meeting the Prince and Princess of Wales through the charity Heads Together.

A little marathon bag for Audrey!

London Marathon completed & a new Guinness World Record set!

Showing Mum my Guinness World Record certificate.

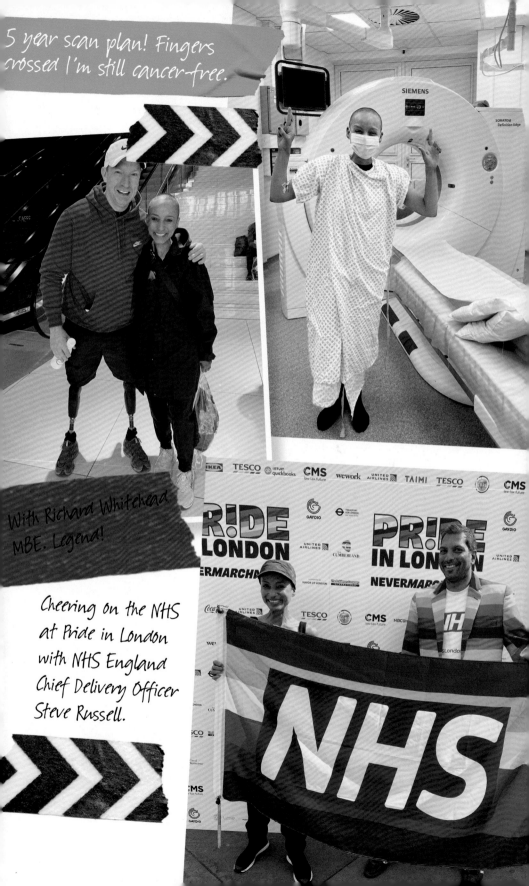

5 year scan plan! Fingers crossed I'm still cancer-free.

With Richard Whitehead MBE. Legend!

Cheering on the NHS at Pride in London with NHS England Chief Delivery Officer Steve Russell.

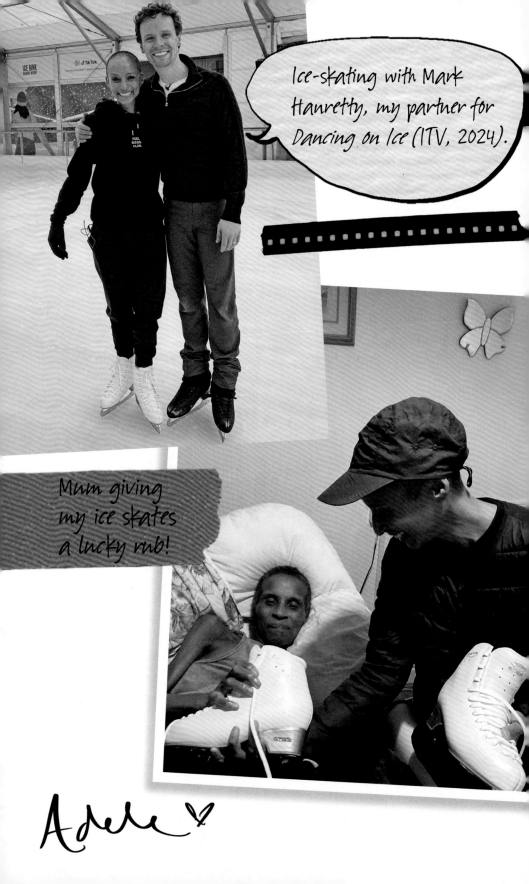

What the mind can conceive the body can achieve.

Lois didn't know she could do the 5K; she just knew she wouldn't give up. Whether she had to run, walk or crawl, she knew she'd give it every last bit of energy she had. Lois lit a fire in me that day. My little sister had done such a beautiful and brave thing for our family. I saved that photo as a reminder of what is possible – a vision of what I could hopefully be in the future.

The very next year, 2017, I was offered another place in the London Marathon to run for the mental health charity Heads Together. I absolutely shit myself. I remember asking Kate what I should do. I didn't run at all at that point, but I had started to work on myself and my mindset. I'd started to read a few self-help books and make better lifestyle choices. My friend Kat had also given me one of her old workout bracelets. It was a stepper thing and it gave you little challenges every day. I made a promise to myself to complete them. It felt good to keep a promise to myself. It was only a small gesture, but it was an important one. Isn't it sad that we're usually the first ones we break our promises to? I didn't want to keep being my own 'let down'. The more I started to keep my promises, the more I started to trust myself. Bit by bit, I had proof I could change. A little walk a day helped keep my doubting demons at bay.

Even though I wanted to make an excuse and say no to the marathon, I had a niggling feeling in me that I should say yes. I still felt so much regret about not doing the London Marathon all those years ago after *Big Brother*. I felt so bad. I'd let that charity down. I could have done a lot of good there, but I had chickened out. Not this time. I loved the charity Heads Together and everything they were about. They do fabulous work and it made me so proud to be part of their team. Plus I had a reason to run – I had someone to run for. My cousin Michael had recently passed away. He'd taken his own life. He was just 19. I couldn't imagine what his mum and dad were going through. My heart hurt for them so much. I'd see his sister Yasmin posting about him on social media. She was so courageous. She was using her platform to spread awareness, help others and honour her brother at such a devastating time. I wanted to help too. I knew the good that charities like Heads Together were doing, the lives they were helping to change and save. That was my motivation, my reason to run. For you Michael, for you Yasmin, for you Uncle Stephen. For all of you. And I guess for me too. Thank you for giving me a reason to run, and thank you to Heads Together for allowing me to be a part of your team that year.

I'll never forget a piece of advice I got before I began training: 'A marathon is 80 per cent mental.' When I first heard those words from my friend Ian, I smiled politely at him and nodded; I acted like I understood. I didn't. I hoped he wouldn't pick up on the confusion and sheer panic on my face. I was unfit and out of my depth. I'd tried a five-minute run on a treadmill and nearly passed out. I hated it. How was I going to do this? *It's all right for you, Ian*, I thought, *you love running. You're built like a runner! God wanted you to do it. He gave you those fabulous legs.* It seemed that Ian actually enjoyed running. Hmmm . . . well, I guess some people like liquorice. *You must have to be born that way*, I thought. *I can't do this. I'm just not that type of person. Bless Ian. 'Eighty per cent mental?' I can't just think my way around the marathon!*

At the time, I didn't understand what he was really saying to me. If you think about it, though, everything you've ever done in your life, everything you've ever achieved, began with a thought. Whatever we think about ourselves sets the limit – high or low – on what we can achieve. As humans, we like to be right, and so our subconscious is always working away to make our thoughts come true. If we don't think we can do something, we'll usually prove ourselves right. So, in a way, I was correct; that version of me then *couldn't* run a marathon. I had to become the person who could. That's what the training is for. Maybe even the great Paula Radcliffe couldn't do a marathon . . . until she could. I've worked on myself A LOT since that day. Yes, I've transformed physically, but I've also fundamentally changed the way I think. That's the difference. You can't change your life without changing the way you think. And I needed to choose better thoughts – I had to change my mind.

To do something you've never done before, you have to become someone you've never been before.

Back to my phone call with Beth. I was supposed to be helping her out by thinking of people who might want to run the marathon with Nissan that year. The faintest glimmer of an idea flashed in my mind. Tiny muscles I hadn't used in a long time, since before my surgery, started to twitch. I didn't dare to think about it properly, but the idea wouldn't go away. A fire I thought had long since gone out had started to burn again – belief.

I was still feeling pretty bruised from not making it on to that TV show – the one where my iron levels meant I couldn't take part – but something just clicked. To this day, I don't know what made me do it, but I decided to ask Beth if I could be considered for one of the places.

I just had this feeling I had to ask, I had to give it a try. And if I got a shot at it, if I got a chance, I knew I'd give it my all. I'd try my best – my personal best. That's all I could do. I looked at all the things I had wanted from that TV show and realised I could do them anyway. This was about showing up; it was about me not hiding away anymore and using everything I'd been through for good: getting off my arse and helping, giving back to those who had helped me. I knew it would be something for me to look forward to, an amazing challenge to strive for, something to help my body heal and keep my mind focused. It would light me up inside. It would help me get back on track, and hopefully, it would be something to help change the representation of ostomates in the UK, raise awareness of bowel cancer and show what's possible post-cancer. I didn't need the show to do any of this – the marathon would give me all those things and more. It would be in my hands, it would be down to me. I'd get out of it what I put in, and what's fairer than that? I knew it wouldn't be easy, but I didn't care.

The year had already started and so I was way behind in terms of the training I'd have to do. And I'd not been on a run for a long time. Could I still run? Would I be able to build up my fitness in time? The furthest I'd run since finishing chemo was a 5K (3.1 miles), but that was a long time ago. A marathon is 42K (26.2 miles) – there's a big difference! My iron levels were still recovering, my feet were still battered by the Capecitabine, and I'd never tried to run a marathon with Audrey. Is it even possible to run a marathon with a stoma? Could Audrey do it? More to the point, would Audrey behave? Was I there mentally, let alone physically? Did I have the courage? Could I, after everything I'd been through, run the London Marathon 2023? On paper, everything said no. But, in my heart, I believed I could.

NOTE TO SELF:
WHAT THE MIND BELIEVES,
THE BODY CAN ACHIEVE.

Gonna Fly Now (Theme from *Rocky*)
Bill Conti

CHAPTER 12

'Getting strong now.'

Gonna Fly Now

Waiting to find out from Beth if I'd been accepted for one of Nissan's marathon places got me fizzing; I couldn't sit still. I decided to celebrate with a little run. I didn't even know if I was in yet, but I didn't care – I just wanted to see how it felt and to check I could still do it. I didn't expect to be fast; I knew I wasn't fit, but I thought I'd just take it easy and go for a little trundle. I aimed for a run around our local park. The route is just over a 5K. If I could do that I'd be happy, I'd be proud. The course consists of main roads, good paths, a set of toilets in case I needed to stop, and a little hill section thrown in there for good measure. Audrey was strapped in her running belt and behaving herself. I had my disco tunes on – Audrey loves disco – and off we went, sashaying around the streets of North London. It was bloody lovely! I was very slow, but it felt good to be back. I was so happy. The way I was feeling after this first run, I'd be lip-synching and drag racing my booty all the way to the London Marathon start line. Hair, heels and all. Beth called – I'd been accepted. Yes!

Then I got Covid. FFS.

Just as I was about to start training for the race of a lifetime, my body held together on a wing and a prayer, I got Covid! And as anyone who's still recovering from chemo and cancer will know, your immunity is knackered. It took me a whole ten days to stop testing positive. By the time I'd recovered it was February and my lungs were rattling now too.

So there I was: the 5th of February 2023, about to start the first long run of my training, Audrey safely strapped in my running belt, big boaty trainers on to protect my feet and the promise of a hug from Kate when I got back home. I was 11 weeks out from the London Marathon. Two of those weeks would involve tapering and winding down, so essentially I had nine weeks to get fit. I should have had at least 16 (that's the advice for someone classed as 'intermediate' too, which I certainly did not feel!). I'd lost five weeks of running time in January.

I tried not to get too downhearted. I was late to start training anyway; what difference would ten more days make? I'd take my chances. I now had the knowledge that I could at least do a 5K, and I might not have been out and about pounding the streets, but I'd been training by stealth. I'd been training for this marathon my whole life – with chance, circumstance and, most recently, my mum as my coaches. She'd just given me a proper good sesh over Christmas. She'd eaten fate for Christmas breakfast! And if her example was anything to go by, I had nothing to lose. Only gains.

That was enough to give me the hope to persevere. My first job: find a plan and stick to it. I went to the old faithful London

Marathon website. It's great – there are training plans on there for runners of all abilities. It's so welcoming, full of tips and advice, and the running plans are downloadable for free. I found the one most suited to me, jumped to week six and started typing all of the sessions into the diary app on my phone. This is my little ritual – if I do this I know it's *on*. Voilà. It was set in stone.

It's that simple for me. This is one of my biggest motivating factors: deciding. It's a powerful act. It's not necessarily the training plan itself; it's the decision to do it. I commit. No excuses. When I decide to do something, I feel it in my gut. It's the proof to me that I mean what I say I'm going to do. If I don't download the plan, then I know I'm not serious and I'm lying to myself. And boy do I lie to myself. I'm sneaky. I'm peevish. I know it might not seem like it, but I am the laziest runner you'll ever meet. There's a side to me that seriously can't be arsed. I think there's still a part of me that low-level hates it. Over the years, I've changed. I am so grateful now that more of me likes running than doesn't. I'd say I'm about 85 per cent on board, which is great – I'll take those odds!

Decide: to settle something, to solve or to conclude. To give victory to one side. One notion. Derived from the Latin verb decidere meaning 'to cut away, to cut off'.

I'd already decided. There was no room for doubt. I wouldn't lie back and let circumstance dictate my life.

Once you decide to do something – and I mean really decide; when your subconscious matches your conscious thoughts, when the fibre of your being aligns with your mind – you cannot be stopped. Deciding cuts off every other eventuality. It's done. It is written. It's happening. And I believe the universe moves heaven and earth to make it so.

This was it – the perfect opportunity, a catalyst for change. I knew this marathon would change the course of my life. I knew it would change me. It would tip the balance back in my favour. The marathon helped me become the sort of person who puts the work in. I'll be honest: I hated it at first – being lazy is so much easier! Many years of half-arsing it are hard to undo, but as the weeks went on and the change started to happen, I became fitter and happier and more of the old me. She was still in there; I just had to wake her up. I like her a lot more. She's much more fun. She's happier, healthier and more excited about life and the future than ever. I hope she stays.

Time to put everything I'd learned into practice and turn this battered, broken and bruised body into a world-beater. Get ready – it's time for my favourite bit of any story . . . It's the training montage! Cue *Rocky* theme tune: it's time to fly.

Here are some of the lessons and techniques that I put into action that can also help us in the marathon of life:

Train hard, race easy

Now don't worry, you don't have to take this one literally. You don't need to absolutely batter yourself in training. What I mean is that if you stick to the plan, if you're dedicated, if you turn up, if you do what you say you're going to do, if you keep your promises to yourself, it'll pay off every time. I'll be honest, you'll doubt yourself in training – you'll have rubbish runs, you'll have those weeks where you don't feel ready, you'll hate your bum bag LOL . . . you might even have weeks where you can't finish your sessions at all. You may wonder why you started all this in the first place. But that's all part of the process – all part of the journey. This is how you earn your stripes.

You are the owner of one of the most magnificent creations of all time – the human body, complete with an incredible, infinite mind. And, as the weeks go on, your body will adapt – it'll grow stronger – and your mind will tap into energy reserves you never knew you possessed. You may not even feel the transformation week to week – everything just suddenly clicks into place, and before you know it, you're ready. So when you get to race day, and you're on that start line, nerves and all, and you're wondering how it'll all go, all you need to do is take that first step, and the new you will take over. You've been here before, you've already practised. Everything that could go wrong already has. This isn't just race day, it's the greatest victory lap of all time! It's the most unbelievable feeling. A day you can treasure and be proud of. BUT ONLY IF YOU DO THE WORK. You get out of the marathon what you put in. There's no way around it. You can't fake it.

> 'Hard choices, easy life. Easy choices, hard life.'
> – Jerzy Gregorek

This is where you get to meet the real you. If you've been skipping sessions, if you've been swerving long runs, if you've not been pounding the streets and practising with your running gels, you'll find out about it on race day. And believe me, you don't want to find out about it on race day. It bloody hurts! You'll have a runny tummy and you'll be aching and chafing in places you never knew existed. Get it all over and done with in training – you'll thank yourself later, I promise.

Mind over matter

My friend Ian was right. The marathon *is* 80 per cent mental (or thereabouts). I also applied this thinking when I was deep in the throes of chemotherapy. As the days got tougher and my body got weaker, my mind got stronger. I believe the mind is so much more powerful than the body. It can take you to a better place anytime you wish. That magic has served me well over the years.

I was lucky enough to get to interview Paula Radcliffe for my radio show as part of the training for my first-ever marathon. I couldn't believe it. I was getting to speak to running God. What an incredible, inspirational woman. And an absolute UNIT! Mentally, she's a total beast. During her competitive career, even though she was an elite athlete and raced through the streets with ease, her body would have been screaming – especially when she set her world record: 2 hours 15 minutes and 25 seconds to run 26.2 miles. Next time you're on the treadmill, try running at 12 mph or 19 kph. Actually, don't because I don't want you to have an accident. Paula's body would have been working at such a high rate that most of us wouldn't even be able to comprehend it. I can't even sprint at the pace she ran, and Paula did it for 26.2 miles. What a machine. Obviously, she's a very talented woman physically and has trained to a very high level, but one of the main things I remember from our chat is how powerful she was mentally. She knew that was key. Her body hurts like everyone else's. There is no easy marathon. Paula was just able to take her mind to another place and transcend her physical world. She'd take her focus away from her body and exercise her mind in other ways. She'd use mind tricks like counting to 100 and do this three times in a row. She said that when she did this it would distract from what she was feeling physically, and by the time she'd finished counting, another mile would have passed. She'd count the lamp posts along the route or focus on her breathing (she did mobile meditation) – anything she could to tame the physical pain and make her body a better place to live until she'd finished. A lot of elite athletes have honed this ability.

Visualisation

I use visualisation a lot. I think I always have – even as a little girl. It's the quickest way to live the life of your dreams. You can go anywhere you want, anytime you want, and it's absolutely free.

'If you can see it in your mind, you can hold it in your hand.'
– Bob Proctor

One of the most exciting things for me when I'm training for a marathon is imagining the medal. I'm not even joking! Kate laughs at me – she thinks I'm obsessed with medals. I think I just love what they represent. They're the physical manifestation of your thoughts, proof of your belief, a reward for having faith.

When the medal for the London Marathon was posted on their Instagram, I was so happy. I must have played that video at least 1,000 times. 'Ooooh that's a beauty, look at it from the back!' Kate must have wondered what I was watching. I went back to it every day. I studied it. I tried to remember everything about it and then, when I was out on the streets and my training runs were hard, that's where my mind would go – away from the fatigue, away from my dodgy right knee and the feeling that at any moment my lungs could fall out of my arse. Instead of thinking, 'I can't do this' or 'I want to give up', I'd visualise crossing the finish line and being handed that medal. In my mind, I got it and I didn't give up.

Thought always precedes action. It's kind of annoying in a way because when your dreams do come true, there's a little bit of you that already knew. In a way, your dreams are the spoilers to the story of your life. So you might as well make them bloody good ones! Give yourself the best season finale, then set about working on the next. You get to be the director, the writer and the cast. Build your own boxset. Mindflix and chill? (OK I'll stop now, but hopefully you get the picture.)

Boy, did I need visualisation when I was on chemo. Nothing could have prepared me for how it makes you feel. There were so many times that I thought 'I can't do this' or 'I want to give up', but I just kept trying to transcend what I was physically feeling and take my mind to a better place. I also visualised completing my chemo, the doctors telling me it had worked and that I was cancer-free. I imagined how good it was going to feel hearing those words.

Visualisation is kind of like having memories in reverse – seeing what you want in your mind and then acting on it to make it real. It can be applied to absolutely anything; you're probably already doing it anyway without realising. For example, you might have a timer on your phone to count down to your next holiday, imagining all the things you're going to do, all the places you're going to see. Depending on what is most important to you, many of those thoughts will actually happen. You'll turn your plans into special moments and memories which all began in your mind. This may seem obvious – like *of course that was going to happen* – but it's the same principle. You visualise things, and you make them real. In fact, if you look at your camera roll now, it'll be full of things you've visualised in your mind first. Is there a picture of you at your new job? Maybe at the gym? Or trying something for the first time? You did that. Look through the last year of photos on your phone, it's full of thoughts that you manifested.

Your thoughts become your future.

So take care of your thoughts. A lot of the thoughts that used to swirl around my head were unintentional. I used to worry – a lot. Worrying about things is still visualising; it's just visualising the things we don't want. So as the song goes: 'Don't worry, be happy' (if only it were that simple, LOL). What I'm trying to say is, the more you're intentional about your thoughts, the more you attract the right energy, people and experiences into your life.

To me, the marathon is perfect for this – it's much more than a physical challenge; it's a mental one too. This is another reason why training is so important – it's a mental rehearsal for the race itself. It's practising thinking about how you intend the day to go. You can't control what happens on the day, but you can imagine all the things you want to happen ahead of time. I remember when I first saw a marathon training plan and it would say things like 'run for 60 minutes'. I was like, *Run? For 60 minutes? Are you joking?! I could watch two episodes of* Corrie *and make a brew quicker than that!* It really is amazing, though – not only does your body become used to running for 60 minutes, but by the end of it you can run for hours. Seriously! It's incredible.

One of the good things about the longer sessions is that your mind has plenty of time to think. Once I started to get fitter and got into my stride, I began to get more comfortable on those long runs. It allowed my mind to wander and I'd be able to focus on having the most amazing thoughts – especially if I had my favourite music on. I'd run along some of the actual London Marathon route and dream about what it would be like on the day. I'd imagine crossing the finish line. I'd watch YouTube videos of marathon first-timers from around the world. Some of them would sit and talk about their experience; others would actually film themselves on the course. I'd try to match up my training miles with what I'd experience on the day. So, for example, if I knew I was around mile six in training, that matches up with running around the *Cutty Sark*. I imagined how good it would feel when I was doing it for real. It's a powerful thing to do. Not only are you envisaging that you'll make it to the *Cutty Sark*, but you're making it a positive experience in your head before you even get there so that, on the actual day, it feels even more incredible. You make your thoughts manifest. You turn your intentions into reality. You make yourself believe you can do it before you've even tried.

Every training session can be a mental dress rehearsal.

I also tried to see the value in my training no matter what happened – good or bad. I'd try not to get too demotivated if it didn't go how I'd planned. I'd take it as a lesson learned; I'd have a rest, reset and come back stronger the next week, or try something different. On the other hand, if a training run was going well, I'd really go to town, dream big and go for it. I'd imagine running past Big Ben, down towards Buckingham Palace and then turning the final corner to run down The Mall and cross the finish line. Oh, imagine how good that will feel. Imagine collecting my medal. Imagine finding Kate and hugging her with all my might. Imagine being someone who'd managed to complete the London Marathon. I was gassed! As the weeks went on and the training built up, I could really start to see it in my mind.

That's how powerful visualisation is. Your thoughts made manifest – proof of the unseen.

Music is the answer

As you can imagine, this is a big one for me. Words cannot describe how much I adore music. I wouldn't want to ever be without it. It's always been there for me, ever since I was a little girl. It's like my best friend. It's a portal to another world: it can take your mind wherever you want it to go, transcend your reality and transform your energy in an instant. Not only is music a powerful motivator for me, it's also a visualisation super-booster. Me + banging tunes + visualising my goals makes running an absolute dream. I get fired up, it takes over me. I feel like I could run forever like Forrest Gump!

I've got so many running playlists and they're made up of all sorts. As long as it makes me feel good, it's on. I've got dance bangers, disco, hip-hop, RnB, grime, UKG, indie, metal, rock . . . a playlist for every mood I guess. Oh, and the amount of music videos I've dreamed up for myself; thank God I'm the only one who can see my thoughts! I'm seriously good at lip-syncing though, and pretending I'm Chaka Khan, Whitney Houston . . . Meatloaf. It's not just my budding tribute acts that I dream about, though. I often put on an inspirational podcast and get fired up by all the good advice too.

When it comes to long runs, each song must have meaning to me. If I'm flagging, the right song just seems to unlock energy in me. A good tip for the marathon is to ask your family and friends to suggest songs for you. It feels amazing when you're in the race and their song comes on. Their energy connects with yours. You know they're out there on the course with you, guiding you home. So that's a good place to start – try to get 26 family and friends' songs on there: one for every mile. Then take it from there. My playlists are hours long. I just put them on shuffle and go for it. Anything can pop up. I've got 'Stand By Me' on there, which reminds me of my dad, then UB40's 'Red Red Wine' will come on and that reminds me of my mum . . . or Meatloaf's 'Bat Out Of Hell', LOL. I bloody love Meatloaf because of her. She used to play his songs all the time. 'Dead Ringer For Love' absolutely goes off too. I imagine Kate singing that one with me because it's a duet.

As you can see, I can get carried away with music though. So, if I feel like I'm going a bit wild, running a bit too fast, I'll play my 'In My Feelings' playlist which is full of slower tracks. I've got lots of RnB and love songs on there, plenty of Luther, Aretha and Whitney. Quite a few heartbreak songs make the cut too. If it moves me or changes my energy, it makes the list. I can be a boxer one minute and the full cast of *Les Misérables* the next. As long as it entertains my mind, it'll do for me. Before I know it, the long run is over and it's back home to Kate who's making a nice roast dinner. Now that's motivation. Not Kate, edible medals. No offence, Kate, I love you, but I also love a good beef shank too. Visualise the dinner you're going to be eating when the training session is over. That's running fuel right there.

Advertise to yourself
This is one where you can 'set it and forget it'. Advertising to yourself is great because, most of the time, you don't even know you're doing it. Plus, you're being advertised to all the time anyway, so you might as well do it for yourself. It's about consciously

programming your subconscious. It's conditioning your mind to manifest the future you want. It's living on purpose.

We've got an Alexa Echo Show in our front room with a big screen on it. It's brilliant. It's used once a day for Mum's quiz and then, for the rest of the day, it's our vision board. It's everything we wish for, all of our dreams rotating away before our eyes – a constant reminder of how we'd like our lives to unfold, what we really want. It's very easy to forget your intentions and your goals, especially with social media. It's very easy to be on autopilot in the morning and log into apps and go down the rabbit hole, spending your time in a space that might not have your best interests at heart. You're not shown what you want to see, you're shown what the platform thinks you'll engage with. I spent far too long being pushed and pulled around by algorithms. I'd start the day with the best of intentions and then get flung off course. I kept forgetting what I wanted from life. If you don't remind yourself what you want, someone else will do it for you. You're in control of how you start your day and what you see. Protect your energy. I've deleted most of my social media apps from my phone. The news apps too. I have to use my laptop or iPad to access them. I've still got Insta, Threads and TikTok on my phone, but I'll only use them if I feel like I've got something positive to add or say. I try to use them as a one-way window to put out good energy. Apart from that, I don't really go on there.

Every screen you own is a chance to make yourself happy, to inspire yourself; a reminder of what's important to you in life.

Make your own algorithm. What makes you happy? What do you dream of? How would you like to start your day? The screens in our house are dedicated to our friends and family, our favourite memories, our dreams and goals – anything that makes us happy or inspired.

It's so easy to get sidetracked and lose sight of what you really want. Having reminders all around you helps you stay motivated, even if it's just one photo beside your bed or a gallery on your smartphone. It all makes a difference.

As soon as I knew I'd be running the marathon, I not only made sure I typed every single session of the training plan into my phone, but I also filled our house with loads of inspirational images of runners and athletes absolutely smashing it. It rubs off on you, you can't help it. You start to see yourself as the sort of person who runs marathons, even if you've never done one before. You start to change your habits and make different choices. You start to change who you are. You start to make your wishes come true.

Circle of five
'You are the average of the five people you associate with most.'
– Tim Ferriss

Now, while I don't think this is totally true, it's a good one to think about. I don't take this literally. I don't even have five friends, LOL. It's just me, Kate and Audrey most of the time and as great as Audrey is, I'm not actually morphing into a stoma. It's a good notion to have in your head though. Where do you spend your time? What influences do you have around you? Again, you get to choose. I see this one as a good way to surround myself with good energy outside of my family and friends. And the good news is, thanks to the internet, I can hang out with whoever I want. I love hanging out with Oprah – she's so cool and she talks a lot of sense too. She's only a podcast or a YouTube video away. I love her audiobooks. Running + Oprah = inspiration to the max! That's a powerful combination right there.

While I was training, I tried to get inspiration wherever I could. I couldn't really find anyone with my exact unique combination of challenges, but I found people who'd been through similar experiences, maybe those who ran with stomas, people running after having cancer, people running on chemo, people not giving in and getting their lives back together; people reclaiming their bodies and absolutely smashing it! So, whatever you want from life, whatever your goals, pick five people who inspire you, five people living the life you want or five people who have good advice and techniques to help you. Fill your world with their energy. It pays off big time!

Keep the good people you already have around you, but you can consciously add more friends in there too. Have as many positive voices and people as you can in the mix. They might be virtual friends, but their words and energy will still reach you and they will change you.

Spending time at Radio 1 absolutely transformed me. I felt so lucky. I was getting to hang out with the best in the business and being paid to do it. How is this legal please? I might not have even thought about the first marathon I ever did if it wasn't for Radio 1. The opportunity came through their relationship with Heads Together, and I just so happened to be in the right place at the right time. Their Royal Highnesses The Prince and Princess of Wales, William and Catherine, founded the charity alongside Prince Harry, Duke of Sussex. They wanted to use their time to give back, help others and use their platforms for good. They're also Radio 1 listeners too, and the Prince and Princess of Wales even came into the radio studios to wish me luck. How amazing is that? The Prince of Wales told me he used to listen to the early breakfast show when he was a part of the Air Ambulance Service. He used to text the show under a different name and I used to shout him out – you can't beat a good shout-out! They have both kept in touch and were kind enough to write to me when I was first diagnosed with cancer and again when I was cancer-free. It means more to me than they can imagine. Not only because it shows what wonderful, thoughtful people they are but also because they know how important it is to raise awareness of bowel cancer. So make sure you speak to someone if you're worried or this book sparks something in you – it's by Royal Appointment. I still pinch myself at my time at the BBC. I grew so much while I was there. I had incredible, inspirational friends all around me – all with their own talents and abilities. And they can be in your circle of five too. All you have to do is tune in.

Run your own race

Try not to compare yourself to anyone else, whether that's in a race or in life. Don't get spooked if it seems that someone is overtaking you – you don't know how long they've been out there running for. Keep it steady and concentrate on you. Your personal best will be different to someone else's. And it will even differ for YOU depending on where you are in your life. A marathon is a great example of this: every one of the thousands of runners taking part is competing under different circumstances. Some are elite professionals who spend every day training with other professionals at the top of their game. Some are complete beginners who have squeezed training around their nine to five or childcare. Some have a disability. Some have been through an illness; others are *going through* an illness. If all of the billions of combinations of circumstances and genetics and life situations could be taken into account, we might find that one person's seven-hour finish time is actually more breathtakingly impressive than someone else's three-hour finish. It's all relative. The first person across the finish line achieves the same goal as the last – they have both covered 26.2 miles. There may be an overall winner, but there are no losers.

Happy feet

Now, bear with me, this is a running-specific one. If you spend money on anything, get good trainers. Your feet are going to spend a lot of time in them. Keep your feet happy and it'll pay dividends. There are lots of running shops like Runners Need that can give you advice on the best ones for you. They quite often have sales on too so you can get yourself a bargain. For my first two marathons, I ran in Adidas Ultraboost ST. They're gorgeous, like slippers for your feet! The ST stands for stability, which I needed because I don't run straight. The marathon you're about to hear about was a totally different affair. I can't wear any other trainer at the moment apart from the Hoka Bondi X. They are glorious! Without them, I seriously don't know what I would have done. My feet are still so sore and damaged from the chemo that I pretty much wear them day to day too. I've got so many pairs in all different colours. I'm so lucky I found them.

On Your Marks, Get Set

So, brand-new Bondi X bought (I went for canary yellow), new bum bag, new running belt to strap Audrey in, new training plan downloaded, banging tunes on, let's go! If only it was that simple. Training this time around was a bumpy ride. It was tough and was much more than I bargained for. I had a new body that came with its own unique challenges. I was slow, and, as good as my trainers were, my feet would bleed from the rubbing on my tender, broken skin. The longer my runs got, the more Audrey started to suffer too. There was one run I did where she was bleeding from the friction of her bag. I felt so sorry for her. That run really knocked me; I was bleeding and chafing in so many places. My body was falling apart. I had to face the facts and get realistic. Yes, I'd run a marathon before, but I'd never run one with this body. I had to think again and give it the respect it deserved. I'd also never run a marathon while I was recovering from chemotherapy. I'd never run one less than 18 months after life-changing surgery. Of course it would be hard, it *should* be!

I started to wonder whether I could even go the distance with a stoma. Would Audrey last the whole 26.2 miles? I got a lot of hope from one guy I found online who had run a full marathon with a stoma. He was based in the US and was really fast too. I can't remember his exact time, but it was under three hours and he was athlete level. He was so fast he said he had an unofficial world record. *Wow*, I thought, *that's amazing*. Even though I was nowhere near his level, I was encouraged by the fact that it was possible. I thought I could at least give it a go. I read his blog, got a few tips on fuelling my body and went on my way. I remember him saying hydration is very important. A lot of water is reabsorbed into the body via the colon. Mine was still unattached, so a big challenge for me would be staying hydrated and, of course, eating enough fuel on the course to keep my body going. It would be a balance between eating and drinking enough but not having too many toilet stops to empty my bag every five minutes. It's very hard to start running again if you stop too many times. I wanted the run to go as smoothly as possible.

It wasn't until a week later that I remembered that guy had an unofficial record. I got curious. Why hadn't they made it official? I did a little more digging and realised that, as far as I could see, there was no mention of any ostomate on the Guinness World Records website. I was fuming! *Well, that needs to be changed for starters*, I thought, *how can I tell them?* That's when I learned how GWRs work. You've got to register them so they can be checked and verified. So I decided to register my attempt at running the London Marathon with Audrey. I wasn't able to just complete it; I had to quantify it, so I decided to register for the 'fastest female to run a marathon with an ileostomy'. That way, I thought anyone with a different type of stoma could still register with GWR too. I registered on the 1st of March 2023. A couple of weeks later, I got an email back saying my attempt had been accepted. They gave me a guide time of four hours to beat in order to set a new GWR. *What? Four hours? FFS! That's bloody fast.* Even though I'd got under that the last time I'd done a marathon, I had a different body then. I wasn't recovering from chemo then. I'd had the full 17 weeks of training, plus my small intestine wasn't hanging out the front of my body. This time around, I had Audrey to carry, I didn't have a clue what I was doing, my feet were bleeding and I only had nine weeks in total to get fit. I looked at the pace of my training runs to see if I had a chance. I was averaging around 9.15 or 9.30 minutes per mile. I'd so far only managed to complete a half marathon in training too. I was off the pace and I wasn't confident I could even keep up that pace for the full distance. There was no way I was getting under four hours.

Oh well, I thought. *It was a nice thought. Don't stress about it. Just keep going and keep trying your best.* That lasted about ten minutes . . . and then I did stress about it. I was fuming with myself. Here I was trying to get myself back on track, hoping to do something amazing for the ostomate community, and I'd been half-arsing it in training. I'd been taking my sweet time and had not been trying my best. I could have taken it a bit more seriously. I knew there was more in me. I thought on it a bit. What if I really went for it during March? What if I put all of the things I've mentioned in this chapter into play? Could we do it? Me and Little Auds? Should we just go for it? Why not? You never know, a miracle might just happen. I've got to go for it. One last adventure with Audrey before she pops back in.

Cue the music again – turn it right up this time!

I stepped it up, I got serious – I even got my David Goggins audiobook on. He doesn't mess about. He always gives me a good kick up the arse. I also found the toughest marathon runner I could find, Courtney Dauwalter. She does ultramarathons for fun. She's bloody awesome, an absolute animal; she's unstoppable. I could watch her videos all day. I found out that she eats mashed potato and waffles for breakfast (hence the waffles in my bag on marathon day, LOL).

I had a word with myself and just went for it. I did everything I could; I tweaked every algorithm under my control. I flooded all my senses with inspiration. I was careful about what I watched, what I listened to and what I ate. I took extra care with my feet and kept them as protected as I could. Kate would bind them with K-tape and plasters. I moved heaven and earth to give it my best shot. This was it. I wouldn't be doing this again. We were going all-in. It seems the universe wanted to help out too.

One day, I was having a bit of a bad day, my pace was off and I felt really tired. I'd decided to pick a new running route that would help get me through. I planned myself a running tour of

some of my favourite inspirational parts of London to give me a
boost. Audrey had her usual toilet break at the Italian Gardens
in Kensington Park, then we ran past the palace, past the swans
in the lake, through Hyde Park, past Buckingham Palace and
down to the river. Audrey loves Big Ben and the Houses of
Parliament.

I continued my run across Parliament Square, past the statue
of Churchill. I checked the time on Big Ben (I used to look at
him to check my pace, LOL) and then I approached the Victoria
Tower. It's at the other end of the Houses of Parliament from
Big Ben. It's where the monarch enters Parliament if they attend.
As I got closer, a black SUV emerged from one of the entrances.
There was a lady in the front, in the passenger seat, waving at
people. She'd put her window down and was saying hello to the
passers-by. I couldn't quite see who it was, but the people on the
roadside seemed super happy. *Oooh,* I thought, *I wonder who
that is.* The car slowed down as it cleared security and gave me
the chance to catch it up. I looked inside and there in the passenger seat was Baroness Floella Benjamin. AMAZING! I wanted to take a picture on my phone, but I didn't want to take my
eyes off her. And also, it's a pain getting my phone out of my
bum bag. *Leave it,* I thought. *Just take a picture with your eyes.*
She waved at me and smiled. OH MY GOSH SHE'S SEEN
ME! SHE KNOWS I EXIST! It felt incredible. I waved and
smiled back. I wanted to shout thank you to her, but her car
started to speed up. I wanted her to know how good she made
me feel. She was just the person I needed to see at just the right
time. It gave me such a boost.

I ran the rest of my route to Battersea absolutely buzzing – along the Thames, past James Bond's work (the MI6 building) on the other side, over Albert Bridge which is so stunning, through Battersea Park, waved at the big gold Buddha and then on to Battersea Power Station. What a finish line. I LOVE that building. It's awesome. It gives me goosebumps. (I'm a bit weird with buildings; I get a bit obsessed with them. I've also got the hots for the Trellick Tower and The Barbican.) I didn't care if my feet were on fire; I'd just seen Floella Benjamin. I got to Battersea Power Station with the biggest smile on my face. I couldn't wait to tell Kate. I was still thinking about Floella when I looked up and saw somebody else. I couldn't believe my eyes. No way? At that very moment, Eddie Izzard, aka Suzy Izzard was walking across the shopping plaza. She looked so majestic as she strolled by. I wanted to say hi, but I couldn't speak. I stopped in my tracks, took in the moment and then got on the phone to Kate.

Me: 'It's a sign, Kate. It's a sign!'

Kate: 'What is?'

Me: 'Guess who I've seen today?'

Kate: (knowing full well she wouldn't be able to guess) 'I don't know, who?'

Me: 'Floella Benjamin AND Eddie Izzard! How amazing. It's a sign. It's a sign to keep going!'

Was this a sign? Or was it just coincidence and chance?

There is no such thing as a coincidence. Notice how everything in your life somehow leads up to the next moment. It's all connected.

I didn't know if I would be able to complete the London Marathon, but I knew I had to try. I had to give it a go. Just when I was faltering, just when I was doubting myself, I saw two incredible people who have overcome so many obstacles in life and kept going. Two people using their platforms for good. Eddie Izzard, the marathon hero who raised over a quarter of a million pounds for charity after completing 32 marathons and performing 31 comedy gigs in just 31 days. Wow! If Eddie can do that, I think I can at least try one. Floella Benjamin, the shining beacon who lit up our TV screens as children, who has run several marathons to raise money for charity. I used to love it when she took us on a journey through the *Play School* windows. She helped us to believe we could achieve anything we wanted; all we had to do was look out of our own windows and dream.

I think I got my sign – a sign to keep going. Now let's see where it leads . . .

NOTE TO SELF:
RUN YOUR OWN RACE.

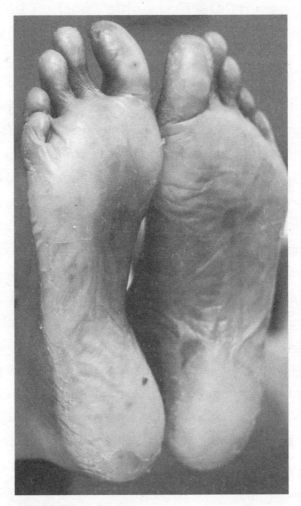

Feet Don't Fail Me Now
Joy Crookes

CHAPTER 13

'I got to stand my ground.'

Feet Don't Fail Me Now

As the race approached, my anxiety snowballed and went through the roof. I don't really sleep well anymore anyway. The constant worry that Audrey will escape from her bag and cause chaos keeps one of my eyes always metaphorically open.

The lovely team at Nissan had put me and Kate up in a fancy hotel just across the river from Big Ben (my new race buddy). We could see him from the foyer. Wow! We had to pinch ourselves. We'd be getting on a coach the next morning and we'd be taken to the start line of the London Marathon. I felt like I was in a dream. I'd never been ferried to the start line before. I felt so lucky.

Kate and I decided to go for a walk after we checked in. She could tell I was terrified and needed to walk my restless legs. We left the hotel and walked over Westminster Bridge towards Big Ben. I wanted to show Kate some of the course and where I'd be running the next day. London looked absolutely stunning as we strolled in the late spring sun. It felt like we were on holiday.

Kate grabbed my hand to lead me through the ever-increasing crowds. I held on to her for dear life. I didn't want to admit it, but I was getting more and more nervous and starting to panic. We were so close now that every mention of the race made my tummy flip. I don't really speak when I'm super nervous. My mind goes blank, I go very quiet and I keep myself very small. If I could have pressed pause and stayed in that moment I would have. This moment was perfect. It was the moments ahead of us that I feared. Had I done enough?

I didn't really feel like eating, but I knew I had to make sure my body had enough fuel in it. Tomorrow would be a day of spinning plates – a constant act of balancing how much food and drink I could consume while running, and how much of it Audrey would be chucking out of me at the same time. I went for convenience, something hotel room appropriate – instant porridge and cold mash; this wasn't just any instant porridge and cold mash though, this was M&S instant porridge and cold mash. Then we nipped back to the hotel room, propped up Kate's iPad with some pillows, took ourselves to Beverly Hills and enjoyed some *Real Housewives*, before it was lights out and off to bed.

Nothing new on race day.

That is great marathon advice. Unfortunately, whoever wrote that hadn't informed Audrey. So there I was at 3.03am on race day, bollock naked. I captured the moment so I could show Kate when she woke up. Lucky Kate! I'd already had a race that morning: me versus Audrey. Moments before I took that photo, I was sound asleep. It was one of those rare occasions when Kate and I were sharing a bed. It should have felt special, a bit romantic even. We could have slept soundly in each other's arms until dawn. Nope. Audrey was hiding in that bed, the little shite-hawk. I was on high alert. No spooning, no heavy petting, no diving. My side of the bed was protected at all costs. I had my washable bed protector complete with puppy pad stacked on top. It wasn't long before the still and calm were interrupted by the tingle. The tingle is the signal that Audrey is about to kick off her bag and all hell will break loose. I woke up, sat bolt upright, whipped off the covers and jumped out of bed. I held my bag on as best I could and ran to the bathroom. I got to the toilet in time – a small victory. Audrey had used last night's tea to wreak havoc. Yep, mashed potato and instant porridge oats sprayed all over me. I took off my pyjamas and tried to wash them by hand in the shower. All the while, Audrey continued to spray her evil concoction out of the front of my body like something from *The Exorcist*. The combination of me being half asleep added to undigested porridge oats and copious amounts of mashed potato made for a sticky situation. It caused a mini dam. I was in one of those fancy floor-to-ceiling showers. I should have got in the bath to clean myself, but the shower was closer to the door. The shower started to flood; mashed potato and porridge goo began to escape under the fancy shower door seal. It poured into the rest of the bathroom, all over the marble floor. It was a nightmare. *I'm too tired for this shit*, I thought. I cut my losses. I turned off the shower and jumped out to try to stem the tide. I spent the next ten minutes drying the bathroom floor with hand towels, spare puppy pads and anything absorbent I could find. I even sacrificed my bath towel. I left the other one for Kate so she could have a nice bath when she woke up. I was naked from the waist down, legs akimbo, cleaning the bathroom floor on all fours. I prayed Kate wouldn't wake up and walk in on me. No one needs to see that at 3am. Or, like, ever.

She didn't wake up, thank God. I put my soggy porridge glue pyjamas in a corner and proceeded to shower myself. I prepared a new bag for Audrey, returned to the bedroom, fumbled in the dark for some spare underwear and climbed back into bed. I lay on my back for the rest of the night, terrified Audrey would do it again. I tried to go back to sleep, but couldn't. I just lay there until 6am, my mind racing, wondering what I was going to do. I was overtired and emotional. It wasn't the start to race day I'd imagined. THIS WASN'T IN MY VISUALISATION! I already felt defeated. I was over it.

The Art of Surrendering

One of the best pieces of advice I ever got was from the lovely Fleur East. I was hosting an event for Girlguiding in Sheffield – the Big Gig. It's a huge annual party which celebrates the Girl Guides and their mentors. It is the sweetest, most pure and inspirational day with fabulous positive energy from start to finish. It's so good it even makes me want kids. Fleur was one of the acts performing on the day. It was the year after she'd appeared on *I'm a Celebrity*, which she smashed, obviously. We had an interview just before her set so she could tell us what she had in store. All of the Girl Guides were super excited. I asked her if she had any advice for this year's jungle campmates. Without any hesitation, she replied, 'Surrender'. I don't know why, but that really resonated with me. *Surrender*. It seemed like a strange word for someone who seemed so fearless and in control on the show. It didn't seem like she'd surrendered at all. I now know what she means, especially as I ended up in that very jungle only a few months later. How spooky is that? I learned all about the art of surrender. You can't control the Australian outback for starters – it'll eat you alive, literally. On reality TV you're never in control. You just have to immerse yourself in the experience and enjoy the ride. I tried to be better this time. I tried to get stuck in and enjoy the experience. But life had bigger plans for me. While my mind was committed to the jungle, my body began to surrender. It surrendered to the cancer within. By shutting down, it was trying to ask for help. That's what I now believe surrender is or what surrender can mean. Surrendering is allowing what is. It's a different tactic in the art of war – it's knowing when to go 'with' something instead of against it until you can find a better way or time to triumph.

I'm so grateful for what Fleur said to me that day and for my time in the jungle. Even though I didn't understand the gravity of what was happening, it must have resonated with me on a deeper level. It led me to get the help I needed. Looking back now, I can connect the dots – all of that had to happen for me to be here today. Everything had to fall apart so it could fall into place.

'Even fallen leaves float in lakes, demonstrating how surrender can hold us up.'
– Mark Nepo

I'm still trying to get better at the art of surrendering. My little mind finds it so hard sometimes. My stupid ego too. LOL. It's amusing for me to look back now and see how irrational I was being. I needed to zoom out. I needed to get perspective. What was I so upset about? I was staying in the hotel of dreams, with the love of my life, about to run the race of a lifetime. I was *in* my dreams. I should have been jumping for joy. So what if I had porridge pyjamas? I could wash them when I got home. I felt like all was lost when I'd already won. I'd made it through my training, and in a few hours, I'd be on the start line and I'd be in the race. Eighteen months ago, I couldn't have imagined this day. I didn't even know it was possible. Twelve months ago, the chemo version of me would have swapped places in a heartbeat. I should have been counting my blessings. Instead, I was spinning out and letting the occasion get to me. Maybe that's why Audrey did what she did. It was a little sign from her to get me to STFU, let go and surrender.

Is this a good 'problem' to have?

This is a question I try to ask myself nowadays. I do it all the time, especially when I go into Chicken Licken mode. Do you remember Chicken Licken? No, not the takeaway; the story from school – the story of the little chicken who's hit on the head by an acorn. He doesn't realise it's an acorn. He thinks he's just been hit on the head by a piece of sky. He then loses his shit and goes around warning all the other animals that the sky is falling down.

Yep, I was in full Chicken Licken mode. I should have asked myself, *Is this a good problem to have? Would thousands of other people swap places with me right now? Yes. Are you about to have one of the best days of your life (you big melt)? Yes. Right, well, get dressed, have a word with yourself, get on that coach and enjoy the day. It's supposed to be fun, remember?*

I got dressed, packed my bag, and Kate, Auds and I made our way down to the foyer ready to meet everyone and get on the coach. I tried to act normal, I tried to smile, but I just ended up looking like that poster for the horror movie *Smile* or some kind of creepy clown. Ian Beale eyeing up my waffles on the coach was the least of my worries.

Race Day

We had arrived upon the heath. Blackheath – one of South London's grandest vistas; the home of the Royal Observatory and the Prime Meridian. Where East meets West. An area steeped in history and greatness. London is transformed on race day: train carriages filled to the brim with nervous and excited runners, the smell of muscle rub and fear in the air, thousands of runners pouring out of stations into Greenwich and making their way up to the heath. It seemed as though the whole world was here, eagerly waiting for the show to begin.

Welcome, welcome one and all! Distinguished guests. Children of all ages. Welcome to today's performance, courtesy of your hosts – the world-renowned BBC. And here to bring you all the action, to oversee proceedings, our ringmaster and marvellous MC: Gabby Logan. Welcome to the TCS London Marathon.

The organisers really know how to put on a show: hot air balloons, brass bands, full fanfare and excitement in the air. There were marquees and tents everywhere and, over to our right, the big top. It had its own walkway and little garden. It was a grand affair, plasma screens on the (tent) walls so we could watch the coverage, catering, posh loos, tables, chairs and sofas. A whole tent of Ian Beales. They were everywhere – celebrities and elite runners, walking around like normal people. My legs were shaking as Kate helped me off the coach. She held my hand, partly to try to calm me down and partly so she could grip me and stop me from running off. Into the big circus tent I went. The clown had arrived at the circus. Gulp. Chicken Licken was about to get fried.

Most people would love it in that tent. All it did to me was make my bottom want to fall out. I guess that is pretty normal for me. I generally can't deal with famous people or people I admire. This made doing radio very hard over the years. I don't know why I freak out, I just do. I'm so awkward. If I admire you, I'd much rather do it from afar. I need the 2D version of you, please; I want to see you through a screen – that makes me feel safe. I don't want to see you in 3D, moving and talking. It scares me. Most of my colleagues at Radio 1 must have thought I was so weird. No, Grimmy, I can't hang out or come round to your house, YOU'RE GRIMMY! No, Scott Mills, I can't come to your epic Halloween party. Stop giving me a heart attack. Going to seven different schools, all before I even made it to high school, might have had something to do with it. Just when I'd get comfortable and make new friends, it would end – I'd be at a new school with a new tie and a new uniform, starting all over again. Whenever I'm home, so many people say, 'I used to go to school with you.' I'm like, *Yeah, so did the rest of the North West.* LOL. So I think I must still find it hard to hold on to meaningful relationships. Part of me might feel like it's going to end. Don't get too close or I'll be whisked away. I'm just not good at being social. I'm also too shy. My brain can only deal with about ten people. I've got my family, my Kate, two of my friends who I adore and love, Nat and Fay (and even they'd tell you I hardly see them in real life), and apart from that, I can't cope. I know it's weird, but I just want to put that out there.

So there I was, in a tent full of VIPs, not knowing what to do. I wasn't just freaking out, I was shutting down and also super nervous about the race. My terror glands were out of control. I needed to calm down. My usual modus of operandi is to do the non-stop nervous wee trick. I usually do this until the race starts. You get in the queue for the Portaloo, have a wee and then go to the back of the queue and do it all over again. Repeat until the race starts. As you can imagine, I'm not the only nervous person on the heath – the queues for the loos are massive, so by the time you get to the front, you're ready to go again. That's out on the heath, though. Not in the VIP tent. Oh no, they've got special loos just outside, with mirrors and sinks and reed diffusers. You even need to go up little steps to get in them. There's still a queue, but it's much shorter and it's got Mark Wright in it. Great! Now I can't even go to the loo. I had to pick my moments – I kept circling the area until it was safe.

At one point, it started raining. *Yes! Kate, let's go, the queue's gone down.* Kate was such a gentleman – she not only accompanied me to the loo but also held an umbrella over me as we walked. I love it when Kate gets butch. She just takes over and tells me what to do. I obliged. I nipped in, did a nervous wee, checked Audrey was still in her running belt and exited as quickly as I could. When I emerged, Kate was not only standing outside waiting with the umbrella, but she was also holding it over Natalie Cassidy's – aka Sonia from *EastEnders* – head. OH MY GOD! I freaked out. My eyes went straight to the ground. Don't make eye contact. *Kate, I don't care if I get rained on, you're going to have to stay out there with Sonia from* EastEnders *until she's finished. Don't let her get wet.*

Too many famouses and not enough places to hide. I was trapped. They kept coming in droves. The tent was getting more and more rammed. I even bumped into Louise Minchin at one point. I tried to keep my head down and move out of her way, but no, she was coming over to speak to me. Was I sitting on her seat, did she need me to move?

Louise: 'Hi I'm Louise Minchin.'

Me: *(thinking) Yes I know you're Louise Minchin because you've got Louise Minchin's face. Help!* (Out loud) 'Oh, hi Louise, pleased to meet you, I know who you are, LOL.'

I did a little laugh and a weird sort of curtsy thing. What a douche.

I don't really remember much of the rest of our chat, I was freaking out too much. I wished her luck in the race. She didn't need it. She's Louise 'The Unit' Minchin. She wrote a book about qualifying for the Team GB triathlon team. What a woman.

More time passed, and they were really stacking up now. So Minchin's in there, Mark Wright, Perri Shakes-Drayton, Natalie Cassidy, Adam Woodyatt, the whole of Babs' Army, who were running in memory of Barbara Windsor. Jake Quickenden was milling about dressed as a femur, and outside was the anchor of dreams, the queen of BBC coverage, Gabby 'Glorious' Logan. One of the organisers came over and asked if I'd like a quick chat with Gabby before I started my race. Yeah sure . . . of course I would. I mean, on paper, I absolutely would. I knew it was a huge honour, a privilege – getting to chat to Gabby Logan on a massive platform, raising awareness of bowel cancer, celebrating ostomates and being able to represent the Attitude Magazine Foundation who I was raising money for. It's an amazing opportunity. But in real life, Chicken Licken didn't want it. I was absolutely bricking it. I don't even want to think about that interview. It was a hot mess. I didn't make sense. Gabby was the perfect MC: I was the perfect clown. So sorry MC Logan. I'm also sorry to Scott Mitchell from Babs' Army and Marcus Mumford, who were there being interviewed with me. Oh, they were wonderful. They both spoke so eloquently, so beautifully and from the heart. I felt like I was talking out of my butthole. In fact, Audrey would have been a better interviewee. My brain just wouldn't work. I was in the interview thinking, *What are you even talking about?* Oh gosh, I'm still cringing. Note to self: practise speaking to Gabby like a normal human or just say no. LOL.

I returned to the big top.

Kate: 'How did the interview go?'

Me: (*Shake of the head.*)

Kate didn't need to speak. She nodded in a way that said, 'Don't worry, forget about that now . . . let's get you ready.'

I stood up to put on the final bits of my kit. I could hear the elites getting ready to set off, so I knew it would be time for the rest of us soon – the magnificent 'masses'; thousands of runners from all around the world, from all walks of life, coming together with one common goal: to give everything they've got, make their family and friends proud, make themselves proud and raise lots of money for charity in the process. I unzipped my jacket so I could start to acclimatise to the temperature. It was a bit nippy out, but once I was in the race, I knew I'd soon be hot, revved up and blowing out steam. My running vest revealed the words 'Adele + Audrey' written across my chest. Looking down at it made me feel so much better. I wouldn't be out there alone – I'd have my Auds.

My running vest was also a reminder of the brilliant charity I was running for – the Attitude Magazine Foundation, an incredible organisation that supports the LGBTQ+ community and their families. Their work ranges from helping people living with HIV to children being cared for in hospices, some of whom are living with cancer. It made me so proud to run in their honour. I'd visited Positive East a few weeks before. It's one of the charities the Foundation supports. It's not too far from the London Marathon course and Rainbow Row. It was such an incredible day meeting the team there. The services they provide are absolutely vital to the community they serve, supporting people going through unimaginable and very tough times. It's a safe space for survivors. One of their initiatives, Re:Assure Women's Project, is a specialist programme for HIV-positive female refugees, asylum seekers and domestic violence survivors. The moment I met the team at Positive East, I was even more determined. The goal was set in my mind. No matter how much I was panicking, I knew once I'd crossed that start line I'd give the race my all.

It was time to dress my feet. I knew from training that my feet were in for a battering. Bring on the blood and the blisters! At that moment, Butch Kate, ever my hero, morphed into Nurse Kate. She sprang into action and started taping and lining my feet. It had been a while since she'd had to do that for me. I think in a way she was happy to be back. I looked down at my feet and wished them luck.

When I looked up, I saw Richard Whitehead MBE next to me. What an absolute legend – another one of my heroes. Richard is also an ambassador for Nissan. They do incredible work together to support Richard's foundation. Richard is a double amputee and uses his platform and experience as a Paralympian to inspire and enable others to get active and live their best lives. Richard sees opportunities where others might see barriers. Through his partnership with Nissan and his foundation he's able to donate prosthetics, give support and help change lives. He's a very special man. So there I was being Chicken Licken and worrying about my feet, while Richard was across from me, swapping out his walking prosthetics and changing into his running blades – a cue for me to stop worrying about my feet and give my chicken head a wobble. Richard stood up. He gave me such a kind smile. He could tell I was nervous, but he knew I'd be all right. He'd already given me so much good advice on the coach ride over, including something I could put into practice shortly:

Take your running gels before you need them.

He'd heard all about Audrey and her antics. 'You'll be fine when you get out there,' he smiled. He's won countless medals as a Paralympian and set world records in both the marathon and half marathon. He's never even mentioned that to me either. I've just googled it now so I could celebrate his career and share his achievements here properly. Wow. That's how humble he is. Looking back, I feel like an even bigger tit now.

Richard was whisked away as it was nearly time for him to set off. I was due to start later because of my predicted time. I'd be running with the five- to five-and-a-half-hour group. That was my predicted time based on my pace when I signed up. I hadn't realised then that I'd be trying for under four hours by the time race day arrived.

It wouldn't be long until it was time for me to be chucked into the ring. Kate took me to get some food. She could tell I needed something to settle my stomach. I needed to replace all the energy that Audrey had chucked out of me early that morning. I didn't care about the 'nothing new on race day' rule by that point – that ship had sailed. Kate took me over to the catering area. Anything you could imagine was on that counter. It was like being at the Bellagio hotel buffet in Las Vegas – they even had a chef making pancakes. The sight of all the food made me want to vom. I was too nervous. My running group was called; it was time to go. Butch Kate kicked back into action and went for the best safe bet she could find – a crumpet. That's my girl! She knows me so well. I love a good crumpet. Plus they're easy for me to digest and not too harsh on my tummy. I started eating it on autopilot before she even had time to toast it. Ha ha. It felt nice though. I loved the doughy, dull texture. It felt like I was eating a little bit of stability. A little bit of hope.

'It's your lucky crumpet,' Kate said.

As I stood there, staring into space, chewing my crumpet like a cow chomps the cud, I hoped she was right.

'This is it. Don't get scared now.'
– Kevin McCallister

Time to Go

We were led out of the tent and round to the start line – the pomp and ceremony in full swing. The greatest show on earth had started! Thousands of excited runners were pouring over the start line: some whooping and cheering, some starting their smartwatches, others fully in the zone and keeping their eyes on the prize. We approached the little opening which allowed anyone in the tented area to join the race. It was about 50 metres before the official start, so you had enough time to get into your stride before crossing the start line. There were thousands of people running towards us from the right. *How am I going to jump into that?* I thought. *I'll get knocked over!* They were rampant.

Kate took me as far as she could, then grabbed my arm, pulled me close and kissed me on the side of my head. I didn't want to let her go. 'Good luck, baby,' she said. 'Don't worry, you and Audrey are going to do it.'

I couldn't speak. I just nodded; everything seemed to be happening in slow motion now. I also couldn't get my phone to work. My running app was frozen. I didn't have time to sort it out so I started a workout on my watch and hoped for the best. I opened Spotify and picked a random song off my running playlist, walked to the vast flow of runners, spotted a gap in the stream and leaped. Within moments, Audrey and I were crossing the start line of the London Marathon 2023.

We were on our own. *Just me and you now, Audrey.* And of all of the songs to randomly pick . . . Drake's 'Make Me Proud'. I looked back towards Kate. All I cared about now was getting back to her and doing just that – I hoped I would make her proud.

I always try to steady myself for at least the first mile. It's very easy to get carried away and run too fast. You've got to get it right, it's a delicate balance. If not, you hit the dreaded 'wall'. I think I may have hit the wall during my first marathon. I may have got a little overexcited and set off too fast. I think I started paying for it around mile 20 when my legs felt like they'd fallen off and my lungs like they'd collapsed. It's the most bizarre feeling. Your body just shuts down around you. You end up doing a weird kind of truffle shuffle to the finish line and hope you don't crash before the end.

'Slow down, and then slow down again.' That's my mantra. I couldn't run too fast anyway, the course was rammed. It must have been an awesome sight for the helicopters above – a big, colourful cacophony of excited runners pouring from the top of Blackheath, down towards Woolwich. I was at least 20 minutes behind the official start of the race. It meant I could ignore the big clocks and not worry about my time. All I cared about was staying steady, staying safe and getting back to Kate. I broke down my goal into stages. If I managed to get further than the 21 miles I'd done in training, I'd be over the moon. If I managed to actually finish the marathon, I'd be on top of the world. I didn't worry too much about the GWR attempt at that point. Audrey and I had a lot of running to do before that. If it happened, it would be the sweetest cherry on a massive cake, but we had to build the cake first.

I noticed some of the Babs' Army runners just ahead of me. I'd heard Scott speak to Gabby beautifully about what running for Barbara and the charity meant to them. I shouted good luck and applauded them as I ran past. They were running as a team, dedicated and ready for the challenge ahead. It was inspirational to see. I remember noticing Natalie Cassidy, hat on, headphones in, eyes focused forward, pumping her arms and fully in the zone. Go on, girl! Seeing her gave me a boost.

As I started to run, I started to settle. Running has that effect on me. It's as though my body moves from the physical plane to another realm. My body takes over the reins. It's like, OK, *we've got this; we'll do the running, you go off and play.* And that's that. My body runs for me and my mind is free to do whatever it wants. I thought of Kate, I thought of my mum. I hoped she might remember I was running today. I hoped she might be thinking of me. I also hoped her nurses wouldn't start playing her Billy Joel and steal my music. If we both use Spotify at the same time, Mum's device wins and mine goes silent. I decided to play it safe and switched over to my Tidal music account. I'd copied my playlist onto there just in case.

My strategy was built around Rainbow Row. It features twice: Once at around mile 14 and then again at mile 21. I couldn't wait. It would be like going to Pride twice on the same day! Traditionally, a lot of runners treat Tower Bridge as halfway, which I totally understand. It's an awesome sight to behold and even better to run over. When do you get the chance to run along the middle of Tower Bridge without getting run over? The crowds lining each side are next level too. It makes for one of the most special parts of the course. The human wall of sound washes over you, it lifts you – but it's very easy to get carried away and use up all of your energy. I decided to use Rainbow Row as my mental halfway instead – not my first visit at mile 14 (which is just over halfway in miles); I'd savour that marker, but I'd wait, I'd be patient. My second visit at mile 21 would serve as 'halfway' for me. I know that sounds absolutely nuts, but please bear with me: if I could make it to mile 21 and feel good, it would be such a mental boost for me. That was my limit in training. I was ready to drop at 21 miles. If things went well today and I kept steady, I might feel like I still had energy; I might not feel like I was falling apart. Add to that the atmosphere of Rainbow Row and seeing all my friends. It would make for the energy gel of dreams. Fingers crossed my plan would work. But that was all waaaaay ahead of me. I'd only just begun.

I imagine the marker for the first mile as my 'proper' start line. It's my version of the 'Go' square on a Monopoly board. The first mile helps me settle the nerves and get into my stride. My internal GPS system had been set. Head for mile six. The *Cutty Sark*.

It's a great feeling emerging from Woolwich and entering the grand boulevard of Maritime Greenwich. The course widens as thousands of runners flood the streets and pour down towards the Thames. If you looked up, you'd see that we were only about two minutes down the hill from Blackheath, the start. We could have rolled down faster! But this is the marathon and you've gotta earn these sights. In fact, you're part of one of the greatest tours of all time. You're running through a World Heritage Site. If you look to your right, you'll be passing the birthplace of Henry VIII, formerly Greenwich Place, now the home of the Old Royal Naval College. You might recognise it from *Four Weddings and a Funeral*, *Lara Croft: Tomb Raider* or an M&S advert – all filmed there. It is a magnificent site on the banks of the river designed by Sir Christopher Wren. If our tour wasn't breathtaking enough already, we're about to see our Madonna on the rocks – ship ahoy! You can hear the *Cutty Sark* before you see her. Well, the roar of her crowds – all adding to the anticipation. It looks as though the course is converging and about to reach a dead end, but it's actually turning as we veer to the right. And there she is – revealed in all her majesty, the grand dame with the copper bottom, the fastest ship of her day: the *Cutty Sark*. Built for speed and carrying precious tea, now marooned on the streets of London, towering over Greenwich like a giant. Shiver me timbers, she's a beauty. I always feel like one of the Goonies when I see her. That perilous bit of the movie when they are spewed out of the water rapids, wondering what fate has in store for them and then are rewarded with the ghost ship of treasure.

Onwards we go, me hearties. On towards Deptford, Surrey Quays and KFC. I always make a note to visit that KFC on the hill. It looks like a really good one. It's got a drive-through and everything. Just up from KFC is the Sophie Raworth Maccies. It's further on in the course, nearer the quays. Yes, there's a McDonald's that reminds me of Sophie Raworth. I saw her there once – I'd set off too fast and was paying the price. I was already knackered. All of a sudden, there goes Sophie, darting past me like a gazelle on an afternoon jaunt, zipping into gaps, bobbing and weaving her way through the weary runners like me.

You go through so many emotions during the race. It really is like life condensed into one long run. You go from feeling on top of the world and like you can achieve anything, to doubting yourself and thinking you'll never finish. At moments, you're fizzing with energy and feel full of beans, then at other times, you feel knackered and want a little sit down. I always try to promise myself I won't stop unless I have to. I'm like a freight train – I take a while to get going, but once I'm on the tracks, there's no stopping me. I'd run through walls if I could. You also experience a range of emotions: seeing the other runners, hearing heartfelt exchanges, noticing the vast range of charities . . . Everyone has a special reason to run or an emotional story. Everyone has triumphed over adversity. Nobody taking part in this is alone. We've all been brought together, to run as one and get each other through. I thought of my mum, I thought of Kate, of my family. I kept checking on little Audrey – she was being an angel. Not a peep out of her. I kept patting her to see how she was getting on with her energy gels and water – so far so good. We were in good shape. My body was processing everything I was taking on board. We were managing to spin the plates.

Soon, we'd be making our way over Tower Bridge and on to the north side of the river. We were currently in Bermondsey. I love running through bonny Bermondsey. It has a special place in my heart. Not only is it an area with so much character and spirit, but it's also the birthplace of the legend that is Jade Goody. I took out my headphones to soak up the atmosphere and hear the voices. It made me smile. It reminded me of her so much. I might not have known her for long, but I'll never forget her. She told me so many stories about all the wild and funny things she used to get up to here. She cracked me up so much. I could tell how much she loved her home; I love it now too. Whether I'm passing through it on the train or running around the streets, I look to the sky and think of Jade. The front of Bermondsey station was absolutely rammed that day; it was an incredible sight. If I could have taken a picture of that moment, I would have. It moved me so much it nearly brought me to tears. They did you proud, Jade – Bermondsey out in full force for you.

Right, that's our tour of the south pretty much done. Let's traverse Tower Bridge and on to the north. Soon we would be officially halfway through the race (the real halfway: 13.1 miles, not my weird made-up halfway). I was absolutely buzzing! And I knew that once I caught sight of the balloons bobbing on Rainbow Row, I'd have done around 14 miles. I'd be *over* halfway. Get in. The race was far from over, but I was encouraged by the thought. Eventually, I spotted the bright rainbow balloons and could hear the joyous music and sound of drag queens in the distance. *Yaaasss! I'm nearly there. Look out for Beth, where's Beth?* I hoped I'd be able to see her. I frantically scanned the crowds to see if I could. It's hard to run and spot people at the same time. You should get a bonus medal just for that. OMG, I found her. 'Beth!' I screamed. I could have cried. She saw me and waved. I was so happy. None of this would have happened without her. I was literally running through my dreams thanks to her kindness and thoughtfulness, her belief in me. I could have jumped into that crowd and kissed her. But that's wholly inappropriate and totally not OK. I think I was the only runner cheering the crowds back, LOL. I was so happy with my Beth sighting. *It's a sign*, I thought. *It's a sign you can do this. Now get yourself through the Isle of Dogs and back round to the other side as safely as you can.* I knew that the next time I'd see Beth, I'd nearly be home.

Ah yes. The Isle of Dogs. Beware the Isle of Dogs! It bites. I still shudder at the thought of it. I don't know why, but it's my kryptonite. The wheels always seem to fall off in there. It's the part of the race where the doubt really sets in and I start to feel the fatigue. My mind isn't 'elsewhere' or 'dreaming big'; it's right here and it's usually screaming. I don't know if it's the gradient or the thrill of the race catching up with me, but my legs turn to lead and my lungs feel like they're about to drop off. I had a car once where the exhaust fell off; it sounded terrible – that's how I sound in the Isle of Dogs. Like an old banger with no exhaust. I usually pray for people handing out Haribo around there. Nobody today, unfortunately, but I still had my strategy: Stay steady, conserve your energy and just thug it out. I was still executing Richard Whitehead's energy gel strategy – lots of fuelling and drinking, but the constant topping up of energy stores had finally caught up with me. It was time to nip for a wee.

There are loads of Portaloos along the marathon route, which is great. You just need to decide which ones you're going to attempt to stop at. Stopping in the race is tricky at the best of times. It's not only hard to manoeuvre out through the other runners, but personally, once I've stopped it's very hard for me to get started again. It's also quite difficult to find a toilet that isn't otherwise engaged – after all, you're out there with thousands of other nervous bladder owners. A good tactic is to spot the loos ahead of time, indicate your way out to the edges of the runners and then find a loo that's free. Not as easy as it sounds. I kept wanting to stop, but not finding the right window of opportunity. We passed a small bunch of Portaloos on the left, but they were all full. Then, just at the end of them, there was an accessible loo. It looked free. Should I? Should I turn back?

Old me, definitely not. Before I got Audrey, I'd only ever used accessible bathrooms to help my mum and sister go to the toilet, never for myself – not even at night-time when I was doing radio. My 'colleagues' (let's face it, the lads) on the other hand . . . they bloody loved it in there. They'd treat it like their throne room. I'd always see security guards, cleaners and others who should know better emerge from the accessible toilet. They'd pretend to look on their phone or sheepishly to the ground if I caught them. Since becoming an ostomate, I am now the proud owner of a golden radar key. The radar key scheme means I can get access to accessible toilets when out and about. It's been a god-send, especially with this little wildcat in my pants. I didn't need my key for this toilet, but should I turn back to use it? I pondered for a few moments. I didn't know when I would get the next shot at one that was vacant. I went for it – I made the break! I turned on my heels and ran back towards the loo, praying it was still free, freaking out all the other runners in the process because I was running the wrong way.

I got in there as fast as I could. I'd practised toilets in train-ing, but not Portaloos and not under duress. Time was of the essence. I had to get my kit off as quickly as I could. I turned, ready to pull my pants down and sit as fast as possible. That's when I realised someone had pissed all over the seat. LADS! FFS! I'd forgotten to bring a pack of tissues so all I had was a tissue and wipe pack from KFC that Kate had had in her bag. You know, the ones they give you with your takeaway. It had a pack of salt in there too. LOL. Unfortunately though, my tissue and wipe set was no match for the pissy seat. Was there any toilet roll in here? And there, to my heart's delight, over in the corner, was a dog-eared roll of toilet paper. Thank you, Jesus! I picked up the roll, made a tissue mitten and proceeded to dry the seat. Who'd have thought I'd be cleaning a Portaloo, on the Isle of Dogs, in the middle of a potential GWR-setting marathon attempt? Not me, but there I was. Oh the glamour. I cleaned the seat as quickly as I could, did a number one, sanitised my hands – twice – and got the hell out of there. Back into the throng of runners, back into the race of a lifetime and into the heart of the financial district, Canary Wharf, with its soaring silver high-rise statues. It's like the TV show *Succession* made manifest. I bet there are helipads on top of those buildings. I always imagine Roman Roy up in one of the towers, in his penthouse suite, looking down at all the runners, probably with pure disdain in his eyes.

On we go again, through the soaring silver birds of Canary Wharf and down a ramp towards the historic and iconic Billingsgate Market, the UK's largest inland fish market. Next up, the weird and wonderful Traffic Light Tree sculpture on Billingsgate roundabout. It's a tree structure made up of real, life-sized traffic lights. They flash constantly. It's confusing at first. *Should I stop or should I start? Should I stay or should I go?* All of the traffic lights flash all of the time – it kind of messes with your head. The Green Cross Code is so ingrained in me from school that I feel naughty running past it. It's worth doing the marathon just to experience that.

Not too far from there it's time to party and shake a leg at the mighty carnival rave that is the Run Dem Crew. Oi oi! By far, they have the best sound system of the marathon for me. They play absolute bangers. I even got a wave off a lady squeezing an air horn. Whoop whoop! Fully boosted, we continue, left around the corner, under the bridge and onto hallowed turf, the colourful road of Rainbow Row. Part II, second visit. Get in. We did it, Audrey! I was so emotional – this is it, I thought. Slow and steady had worked, and by the grace of God, I still felt good. I didn't feel like collapsing this time; I felt amazing. It was time to put everything on the line, switch on the afterburners and go for it. Run to Kate and take it home.

I ran with everything I had. I ran for everyone who'd helped me get this far, everyone who'd believed in me, everyone who'd been kind enough to donate. Everyone who'd inspired me, everyone who'd shared their story to help others. I thought of the angels of the NHS, the stoma squad of Great Ormond Street Hospital. My family, my friends, my Kate – the invisible force between us helping to draw us back together. Seeing her would be my prize. I hoped she knew that, without her, none of this would have been possible. The thought wouldn't have entered my head. In fact, I don't think I'd have found the tumour in time. Without her care and unconditional love, I don't think I would have worked on myself. I would have stayed in the depths of mourning, my soul asleep, sleepwalking through life. It's never too late, you know. It's never too late to start again. Here I was at the age of 44, getting my life back and fitter and happier than I was at 24.

I raced past the Tower of London. I ran as fast as my little legs would carry me, down Embankment and on towards the London Eye, the tower of Big Ben in front of me. Here I was again. I was back in the place where I'd walked so nervously less than 24 hours before. What a difference a day makes. I couldn't imagine all of this yesterday.

'Today is the tomorrow you worried about yesterday.'
– Dale Carnegie

Today, the road under my feet signalled there was less than a mile to go. I was so elated and so engrossed in the atmosphere and my surroundings that I wasn't paying too much attention to my music. My Bluetooth headphones are getting old now and the battery on the left one had run out a while ago. I was down to just one. I could barely hear the music. But then a miracle. Of all the songs to start playing, of all the songs out of the hundreds I had on my playlist, one came on about overcoming the odds and giving something your all: Whitney Houston's 'One Moment in Time'. It was the perfect song at the perfect time. I got goosebumps, I gasped. It took my breath away.

Serendipity was serenading me home. I looked up to the sky and thought of Auntie Maxine. I knew with all my heart that she was with me. She was playing Whitney for me, she was carrying me home.

I felt like I was flying right down Birdcage Walk, all the way to Buckingham Palace. I don't even remember my feet touching the ground. If you saw someone levitating down there, it was me – I swear. Whitney gets me every time. With every beat, every lyric, every note, she fills my soul. I heard the roar of the crowds as I approached Buckingham Palace. It was picture-perfect: the great palace to the left and tiers upon tiers of wonderful crowds to the right. Union Jack flags were proudly flying and lining the red road of The Mall. This was it – the last 200 metres. That's when I saw Richard. He was waving at the crowds and getting them going – the sound was incredible.

How could this even be? Of all the people to see, at this time in this place – when we'd set off completely separately, when I'd stopped for a wee – someone who had inspired me and helped me earlier that day. I couldn't believe it. I went to run over to him to give him a hug, but then I remembered, *Shit. The record. You don't know what your time is. RUN!* I shouted to Richard and waved at him as I ran past. He turned and gave me the biggest smile. I hope the master was proud of his student. I was nearly there. I wanted to run with Richard, but I also wanted to finish the race before Whitney stopped singing. LOL. I was living in my dreams. I knew I might never get this chance again. And I kid you not, as the song was about to finish, I crossed the line . . . with 12 seconds of the song left to spare. AMAZING.

We did it, Audrey, we really did it! We're home. That's when the emotion hit me and I burst out crying. I couldn't comprehend what had just happened. All the dots had connected, all the stars had aligned – from hospital bed to the race of a lifetime, all within 18 months. It was a miracle.

It is not the marathon you conquer, but yourself.

True, true. If you believe it in your heart, and you have the courage to try, you can achieve it: mind over marathon each and every time.

I needed to find Kate. I needed to hold her tight and just cry. I was so happy. The next few moments were a blur. I know I got to speak to my amazing friend Matt. I was also given my medal. Yes! I somehow found myself on TV again, in the presence of not only Glorious Gabby Logan but also Superwoman Sophie Raworth. God knows what I said to them. Dear Gabby and Sophie, please take this as a full and sincere apology if I was a complete babbling idiot and I didn't make sense. I think the only thing stopping me from having a nervous breakdown was the fear of the cameras and also wanting to know my time. I hadn't paid attention to the clocks because I had set off late and my smartwatch is a little blagger. I don't trust it. I only believe my time when it's on my phone. Had I got under four hours? I kept asking people, but nobody was able to tell me. They're hardly standing there checking my time – they've got jobs to do! Sophie kept saying she thought I'd got under four hours, but I wasn't sure. I know she does the news so she tells the truth, but I'd set off late and I'd cleaned a Portaloo. What if my time was four hours and one minute? I'd still be proud I'd finished, but I'd also be raging at the person who'd pissed all over that seat. I noticed Gabby holding her earpiece and nodding.

Gabby: 'Do you want to know your time?'

Me: 'Yes, please . . .'

Gabby: '3 hours, 30 minutes and 22 seconds . . .'

Me: 'What?!'

3 hours, 30 minutes and 22 seconds. WTF?!

How? How? It's not possible. That time was faster than I'd ever run the marathon IN MY ENTIRE LIFE. Faster than when my intestine was still inside my stomach. I couldn't believe it. As I stood there in the middle of my Gabby/Sophie sandwich, I realised it was my personal best. Wow. I couldn't quite compute it but . . . *I'll take it*, I thought. Gabby Logan has just said it live on TV so they can't take it back. I've got proof. I've got receipts! If they've made a mistake, it's too late now.

I found Kate and she already knew. Kate always knows. We didn't even need to speak to each other. I fell into her arms. I held on to her with everything I had. It was the perfect end to the perfect day. *We did it, my love – you, me and Audrey.* This medal was hers just as much as mine, if not more. Oh, and don't worry about Audrey; Kate had made her a mini medal. It's so cute. Audrey had her own little running number and kit bag too.

It was nearly time to call my dad; I just needed to find an area where I could get a signal. I couldn't wait to tell him, to thank him. I hoped he would be proud. I hoped he would know that I had him and Mum in my heart every step of the way. I hoped he could arrange for someone to get a message to her at the nursing home. There wasn't enough signal to get internet on my phone; otherwise, I'd have been straight on her Alexa to show her my medal.

We just had one more job to do before I called my dad though, just to double-check this wasn't a dream and to make it official:

We had to find the man in the incredible, crisp, navy-blue blazer from the GWR team and take a picture. I found him in a little area near the back of St James's Palace – a makeshift photo booth where you can register your record attempt and get confirmation that you've done it. I joined the most remarkable queue I've ever seen. In front of me was someone dressed as Aladdin complete with a magic carpet. I think there was a Forrest Gump, a milkman and an Eiffel Tower milling around too. It was the most random queue I've ever been in.

Eventually, it was my go. I was careful not to stand too close to the GWR man and his fabulous blazer – I didn't want to muddy him with my 'I've just been running for 26.2 miles' funk. And there we have it. A GWR for the fastest marathon by a female with an ileostomy. Or, if Audrey had her way, the fastest marathon by an ileostomy dressed as a human.

She got bigger cheers than me during the race. Ha ha! People kept shouting *Audrey!* at me because she was written on my vest. She bloody loved it.

NOTE TO SELF:
IT IS NOT THE MARATHON WE CONQUER, BUT OURSELVES.

Finally
Kings of Tomorrow feat. Julie McKnight

OUTRO

'I now have no fear of my fears

And no more tears to cry.'

Finally

Finally, finale, fin, the end. We're here, my friends. Wow, what a ride, what a journey. I hope you enjoyed it half as much as I did sharing it with you. I absolutely loved having you here with me, every step of the way. I'm so happy I got to write it down.

Audrey's already had my pants down this morning, making me tend to her. She's super fidgety at the moment. That's because there's something new on the horizon. It's 5.27am on the 15th of October 2023. It's not yet been two years since I had my operation to remove my tumour. Audrey isn't even two yet. In fact, two years ago today, I didn't know any of this was to come. I didn't know I'd be writing these words into the note section of my iPhone. Isn't life amazing? Who'd have thought I'd be able to write a whole book on a phone and not a typewriter? Who'd have thought I'd be able to write a *book*? Not me. For one thing, I didn't think I'd have anything to say. For two, I didn't think people like me wrote books and for three, I didn't even used to read. My favourite book used to be Facebook.

I only really started reading when I heard one of my friends say that she was doing a reading challenge. She said she was going to try to read 52 books in a year. I couldn't believe it. I also couldn't think of anything worse. Why was she giving herself homework? And enjoying it? Who actually likes books? The only person I know who reads books is Kate. She's got shit loads. She rammed our old flat full of them. She's just joined our new local library to get even more of the little critters. She used to buy me books, especially when I was in the depths of my depression days – God bless her. She'd 'buy them for herself', read them (as if to demonstrate to me how they should be used) and then casually leave them around for me. 'You should read this book – you'll like it,' she'd say. I'd nod and then just end up hiding it in her bookcase with all the other stuff she had bulging out of there. Who's got the time to read books? They take ages and a lot of the time they're not even real. They're just stories someone's made up out of their mind hole.

Slowly but surely though, as I started to turn my life around, began walking with my stepper thingy (that I was given by my friend Kat), eating better food, making better choices, I wanted books that could help guide me. I've had a few books I liked in the past. One of my favourites was Arnold Schwarzenegger's *Encyclopedia of Modern Bodybuilding*. Now that's my kind of book. Reference, facts, technique, answers, wisdom, advice, beautiful photos of a man dedicated to building his mind, body and soul. It was a massive book too – you needed to start bodybuilding in order to pick it up. In fact, when I thought about it, I enjoyed textbooks at school and reference books. Books about science and sport. I loved reading about inspirational people too.

As I walked, I started listening to podcasts of that nature; stories of lives well lived or audio I could learn from. *Desert Island Discs, The Infinite Monkey Cage,* Oprah Winfrey's *Super Soul Sunday, The Tim Ferriss Show*. I then mustered my way up to reading a few of the books Kate had suggested: *Year of Yes* by Shonda Rhimes. That book terrified and excited me in equal measure. I was so inspired by Shonda, but I was also worried that she'd start making me say yes to stuff. I wasn't ready for that . . . yet.

I'd started to subconsciously take things step by step. Start small and build my way up. I'd begun to change the five people I hung out with each day and I didn't even know it. Even though it was mainly listening to new podcasts or finding new people to follow on social media, it opened up a new world for me. I changed what I watched and what I listened to. I even changed what I ate – I started to eat more natural food and less processed food.

> *'Grapes are nature's Skittles.'*
> – Kate Holderness

Kate is too funny! My spoiled taste buds didn't believe her at first, but as I walked more and more each day, ate food that we had made with as natural ingredients as possible, my world started to change. Fruit became my pick 'n' mix; homemade 'healthy fakeaways' replaced my takeaways. Slowly but surely, my misery started to melt away. It all might have been micro changes to me day to day, but it made for mighty macro changes in my life. It was the momentum I needed to change.

I started to love walking so much that I used to walk home from my early breakfast show at Radio 1. I lived about three miles away. I did it religiously after every show, no matter how tired I felt and no matter the weather – I walked in snow, sun, wind and rain. If I had a show, I walked home (even after the 2.15am starts). As I mentioned earlier, I'm probably one of the laziest 'fitness' people you'll ever meet. There's a huge inner sloth residing within me that essentially can't be arsed, so I have to trick myself into working out. Walking home gave me a guaranteed 5K workout every day. I didn't need to join a gym, I didn't need gym clothes. And I could listen to all my favourite tunes or podcasts as I walked. The views were stunning too – I could walk through the historic and iconic streets of London as they woke up each day. I loved seeing people on their way to work or opening shops and bakeries, making their beautiful breads and cakes, stacking the displays in their windows sky high, filling the air with the most incredible scent of pastry bouquets. I knew Kate was at home waiting for me with a hot cup of tea when I needed it and I could reward myself with a little sleep when I got home. Bonus! The perfect start to every day. Now that's my kind of workout, my kind of gym.

The walk would take me about an hour, so I figured that if I

set myself my friend's challenge to 'read' 52 books in a year, I
could easily get through a book a week if I got it on both Kindle
and Audible (I was saving money by not having to get the Tube,
after all). It took me a good three years after she said it, but I still
did it – I listened to an hour of an audiobook each day and
would then read the Kindle version at weekends and, thanks to
the cool 'whisper-sync' feature, I could keep them in sync and
highlight the bits that stood out to me. That's where my 'notes
to self' first started. I'd note down all my favourite things from
my books, the podcasts I'd listen to, posts I saw on social media
and just general things I'd see when I was out and about. I'd take
photos and store those too. It was all in my phone, just a search
away – my own mobile self-help library. No rammed shelves
needed. If I ever got down or overwhelmed, I could go through
my phone, find my 'notes to self' and remember I was just having a bit of a wobble. I'd find the words I needed to read or the
audio I needed to hear to remind me I'd be OK. That reading
challenge transformed me. I read somewhere that a good book
is like sticking your hand in glue: 'Something always sticks.' I
love that. I truly believe it too. I don't think you could ever read
a book and not get something from it, even if it's just a sentence
that resonates with you. That idea or that sentence might be the
thing that changes your life.

Those 52 books led me to where I am right now. I was meant
to hear my friend casually mention her book challenge. It was
meant to simmer within me until I was ready to listen. Everything
that happened, happened at exactly the right time. Cosmic timing is always right. You're right where you need to be and life is

unfolding exactly as it should. Nothing ever meant for you will pass you by. If it's not happening now, it's so something even better can come your way. What you seek is seeking you. And if you're faced with another one of life's marathons, you already have everything you need to take it on and absolutely smash it. It's all within you – it's already there.

That's really what the title of this book is all about: *Personal Best: From Rock Bottom to the Top of the World* (I actually wanted to call it 'No bottom to the top of the world', but the publishers weren't into it). Seriously though, at the start of all of this, it appeared that I was at my lowest point. I was recovering from cancer, my body had been ravaged by chemo, and my intestines were now on the outside of my body. At the other end of the story, I ran a marathon in a faster time than I ever had before, even when I was in what I thought was the best shape of my life. That personal best came *from* my personal worst, not despite it. And it really wasn't about the certificate at the end, the medal or the finish time or any of that – it was about who I became in the process. Something could've happened on marathon day to prevent me from running that race, but I still would have been the personal best version of me that day because of everything I'd been through along the way. If you feel like you're at your rock bottom, just know that your personal best self is inside of you right now. You might even think you can see them, far off in the distance. You know you're going to have to travel a fair bit to get to where they are. You'll set off on a journey to meet them, growing and levelling up along the way so that when you do eventually get to your personal best, you'll realise you've been looking in a mirror all along. It's been you the whole time.

The only limits we have are the ones in our mind.

2021 was one of my greatest teachers. The moment of my diagnosis had taught me so much. It was one of the most valuable few seconds of my life, and that's all it took – a second of time to give me a second chance, the smallest of margins to give me the greatest hope. I felt like I got my life back in that second, the digits back on my cosmic clock. I didn't know how much time I had, I guess none of us do, but before I went into that room I wasn't thinking about the clock. I was pissing my time right up the wall, spraying my minutes around with gay abandon. Thank God I got some clarity. It knocked some sense into me and I was grateful. I had a second chance to spend my time more wisely. Another golden ticket. Another play in the great lottery of life.

OK, so before I get too Yoda on us all and pretend I actually know what I'm talking about and that I've got it all figured out, I haven't – far from it. I can't sleep at the moment because I'm about to start a new 'marathon' . . . one far from my comfort zone, and I'm already absolutely shitting it. Well, it's not a marathon; it's a bloomin' treat; it's a flippin' miracle! It just might take the effort of a marathon for me to get my non-dancey, un-sparkly, wonky, lopsided body on board. So that TV show that I didn't make it on to? The one I didn't have enough iron in my blood for? Well, it was ITV's *Dancing On Ice*. YAASS! The official home of the incredible icons and masters of the ice,

Jayne Torvill and Christopher Dean, along with their fabulous friends. We finally did it, Audrey! We made it on to *Dancing On Ice*. Can you believe it? No, me neither. How the heck did we sneak on? I cannot tell you how happy and honoured I am to have finally made it on to the show. I'm one proud ostomate for sure. I didn't know if it would be possible, if it would ever happen, but I hoped it would. As I've learned in life, things only click into place when the time is right. So I guess my time is now.

I'll be honest, I was heartbroken about not getting on the show previously, but I think that's because it represented much more than a 'no' to me. It felt like cancer had won in a way . . . and I was gutted. But it also helped give me the drive and determination I needed to keep getting better, keep moving forward and making sure I leaned on others for help. I didn't know I had a problem with my blood or that I had a low iron count. Without my treatment for that, I wouldn't have been able to run the marathon. Without that 'no', I wouldn't have this book. Without that no, I might not have made *Dancing On Ice this* year. All through my marathon training I'd watch the show as a boost. It made me so happy; it's such a heart-warming, positive show and the dancers are so beautiful to watch. It allowed me to dream. All of the contestants inspired me. It was a moving, living, breathing vision board for me to focus on each Sunday night and now here I am, actually *inside* of the vision, feeling super lucky and super grateful. It's magical. It's a miracle.

*'What we call the beginning is often the end. And to make an
end is to make a beginning. The end is where we start from.'*
– T. S. Eliot, 'Little Gidding'

Everything that has happened in my life has led me to this point.
My past has prepared me for my present and it's given me hope
for the future. And praise the Lord it has. I've had two master-
classes this week, and two training sessions, and I've already got
my Chicken Licken head on. As much as I've loved this week,
it's also been a baptism of fire. Ice skating is SO HARD. It seems
to defy the laws of gravity and physics. It doesn't make sense to
me. It's practically impossible! Ice skaters are stunningly beautiful and seeing them move across the ice is a joy to witness. It's
spellbinding and elegant to watch . . . and impossible for me to
replicate. What have I done? I've barely started and I'm already
bricking it. I'm *Bricking It On Ice*.

But that's all part of the journey isn't it? I need to remember
that I'm watching people at the top of their profession. Of course,
they're going to make it look easy and effortless. That's why
they're so good at what they do.

I can't tell you how many times I've had to remind myself of
the things I've said in this book – that's how easy it is for me to
forget and freak out. Every challenge we take on looks different,
so I guess it's always worth remembering that, no matter what it
is you're facing, there's always a new way to deal with it, new
lessons to learn. I've got many of those ahead of me and I can't
wait. No matter what happens over the next few months, I
already feel like a winner. However this plays out – whether I get

chucked off in the first week or I go all the way to the end – if I've given it my all, if I learn something, if I'm proud of what I've done, *that* is winning to me. Audrey and I are officially on the line-up of *Dancing On Ice* series 16. No matter how frustrated I get, how many times I fall or how inferior I feel compared to the other glorious, glamorous and gifted contestants, this is a good 'problem' to have. I get to be surrounded by greatness and I get to do it all with little Audrey by my side.

You're freezing your bollocks off? Good!

You've just embarrassed yourself by being dragged across the ice by an office chair (in front of Torvill & Dean)? Good!

You can't skate or dance and you have as much grace as a 'reversing dumpster truck'? Good!

These aren't problems. It's a privilege to be experiencing all of this. It means you're alive. You're getting to spend your days being taught an Olympic sport by the best figure skaters the UK has ever produced. This is going to be one of the most enjoyable and rewarding 'marathons' you've ever had the opportunity to experience. It's going to change you and it's going to change your life. Every person you're about to meet on this journey and everything you're about to go through is a blessing. It's up to you to make the most of it.

As for Audrey, the plan was always to have her reversed after I'd finished chemotherapy. Audrey was there to help my body heal and recover while I was being treated and, once I was cancer-free, they'd pop her back in and I'd start to learn to use my old bottom again. Well, in true Audrey fashion, she's thrown a spanner in the works, the little terror. While it's been healing, my colon has become twisted. I've had a couple of procedures to try to straighten and stretch it out (this involves a balloon up the bum and is way less fun than it sounds), but it's still a bit 'kinky' on all accounts. The good news is that we have made progress, and once Mr Bhan is happy, he'll be coming for you, Audrey!

I don't know what to think about that right now. As much as I know it's important to have a reversal to help me get back to full fitness, I will miss her so much. I know I'll cry. I reckon I'll be heartbroken. This cheeky little sausage has helped keep me going, she's kept me alive. Audrey has given me my life back. She's been my little buddy throughout it all. It'll feel weird without her. At least I'll always have a scar on my body to show where she's been – a tribute to my little Audrey. It'll be the most beautiful kintsugi in her honour. Plus, I know she'll still be there – she'll just be back inside my tummy. Not outside of it causing havoc.

Thank you so much for taking the time to read this book and for being here with me. You've helped me more than you could ever know. In fact, you've actually written it with me. I only knew what to say because I thought of you. I only had the courage to write this because I hoped its message would find you. Putting all of this into words has meant I've been remembering and relearning some of my biggest lessons. I've been learning about myself along the way too. Writing this has made me a better person. It's also enabled me to thank and celebrate those who have helped and inspired me – those who have saved me. Through these words, I hope to help others as

I have been helped myself. Whether there's something in here for you, your family, your friends or your loved ones, I hope you always carry the message with you. Please also know you're never alone. No matter what you go through in life, there's somebody somewhere in this world who's going through the same.

There are angels and heroes all around us; we just need to take the time to notice them.

There's always someone who can help, someone who can relate, someone who can light up your night sky. So, when the journey is long or it seems that all is lost, please always remember the words we've written together.

The first step is just as important as the last.
It's not what happens in life, but how
you respond that matters.
It might not always be perfect, but there
is beauty in imperfection.
You may not always feel brave, but there
is strength in vulnerability.
Dream big, start small.
There is no right or wrong way to do
this. There is only your way.
Keep listening to your gut; the answers are within.
As you progress through this journey, expect
nothing and appreciate everything.

There are no losses in life, only wins and lessons.
It doesn't matter how many times you fall;
it's how many times you get back up.
What your mind believes your body can achieve, so
may your actions always match your ambitions.
Don't compare your journey to anyone
else's; run your own race.
And remember, it is not the marathon you
will conquer . . . but yourself.

NOTE TO SELF:
THE END IS JUST THE BEGINNING.

At Your Best
Aaliyah

END CREDITS

'When I feel what I feel,
sometimes it's hard to tell you so.'

At Your Best

D ad, you are my hero. You have shown me that no matter where you start in life, no matter how much others doubt you, you always have the power to rise within. You are unstoppable. No matter how many times you've been knocked down, you've always got back up. If I achieve half the things you have in my lifetime then I know it will be a life well lived. Thank you for giving me my brothers and sisters, the five best friends I could ever wish for. I'm so happy my mum found you; you will forever be the love of her life.

Lesley, Loren, Les, Lois and Lloyd, I am beyond proud to be your big sister. Thank you to each of you for inspiring me every day to always try my best. Words cannot express how much I love you.

To my Diane and Kaméo, there is no end to the depth of my love for you. You're more than cousins or sisters to me. You will be in my heart eternally.

Auntie Ann, I am so lucky to have you in my life. Thank you

for showing me how to be strong even when it seems all is lost. You are the reason I knew I could get through this. I felt it in my soul. Thank you for helping me. I know Uncle Phil is watching over you, proud as punch in paradise.

Dave and Sue, I love you. Thank you for everything you do for me. You are my family and I love you both with all my heart. Thank you for making the love of my life too – my Katie.

And to my Kate, my true love, the day you walked into my life was the day I was saved. Nothing will ever take me away from you, I promise. I will forever be by your side. In this life and the next. I will always find you. I am not me, without you.

With thanks to my NHS heroes: Dr Yuen, Mr Bhan, Dr Alice, Elaine Cronin, Ann, Maria and Trendelina, and Dr Khurum Khan . . . to name but a few. You are an absolute credit to our nation. Thank you to the whole NHS team, right across the UK, every single member of staff. We are so very lucky to have you. Thank you for saving my life.

Adam Strange – superhero by name, superhero by nature. Thank you for all of your incredible advice and support along the way and for believing in me and Kate right from the start. This book is for you, your family and your beautiful mum. Both you and your mum inspired us to stop playing so small and find the courage to finally trust our guts and sit down and write.

Jamie Brenner, you're such a beautiful soul. You are our sunshine on our darkest days; we love you.

Lauren Whelan, from the moment we met you, Kate and I knew you were the perfect person to bring our book to life. We prayed you'd choose us. It's been a pleasure to bask in your brilliance, you absolute Queen. We hope we've managed to harness some of your wonderful radiant and rampant positivity throughout the book too! I also apologise for all the shits and bloodys throughout the text, but I bloody shitting needed them. We have adored working with you and your incredible team. And thank you so much for introducing us to the mastermind that is Julia Kellaway.

Julia, thank you for your wisdom, guidance, sensitivity, ridiculously sharp brain and for filleting Kate and I the finest fish we could ever wish to dine on. Ha ha . . . here are a load of exclamation marks just for you!!!!!! (Feel free to tweak.)

There are so many people in my heart who I'd like to say thank you to. I hope you know who you are and I hope you know what you mean to me. I would have thanked you all personally, but Kate and Julia are being proper stingy with the word count. So I'll leave you with these words: thank you for helping me achieve my personal best; I couldn't have done it without you.

This book is dedicated to the memory of Jackie Roberts, my beautiful mum. I'm so sorry you never got to hold this book in your hands Mum, but please know you're the whole reason it's here. There is no book without you. 'You're my first, my last, my everything.'

Jackie Yvette Roberts,
01.09.1962–04.01.2024

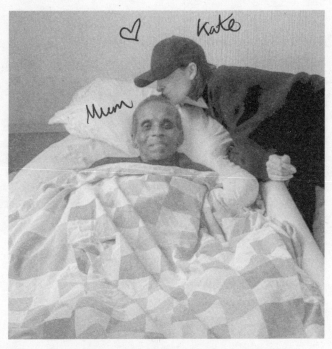

My world. The last photo I took of my mum.

Picture acknowledgements

Most of the photographs are from the author's collection.
Additional sources in 2nd inset:
Alamy Stock Photo: page 5 below/photo Guy Corbishley.
Getty Images: page 6 above left/photo John Philips.
Ken McKay/ITV/Shutterstock: page 1 above and centre right. ©
Shutterstock.com: image on pages vi, 6, 24, 36, 56, 64, 82, 100,
110, 128, 144, 166, 176, 202, 234, 248 and 253.

References

p. 47:   *'Zoom in . . . and observe.'* Rick Rubin, *The Creative Act*, 2023.

p. 51:   *'beautiful poem by Rupi Kaur'*. Rupi Kaur, 'representation', *the sun and her flowers*, 2018.

p. 57:   *'Ask every . . . move on.'* Oprah Winfrey, Commencement Address, Stanford University, 2008.

p. 107:   *'Life whispers . . . a brick.'* Oprah Winfrey, 'Life First Speaks to You in a Whisper', *Oprah's SuperSoul Conversations*, 22 Jul 2020.

p. 142:   *'Be thankful . . . have enough.'* Oprah Winfrey, Facebook, 3 Oct 2011. <https://www.facebook.com/100044572113214/posts/1015037237 8472220>

p. 164:   *'I want . . . with you'*. Tracey Emin, 'I Want My Time With You', St Pancras International Station, 1 Apr 2018.

p. 181:   *'Hard choices . . . hard life.'* Jerzy Gregorek, 'Hard choices, easy life', [n.d.]. <https://thehappybody.com/ard-choices-easy-life-jerzy-gregorek>

p. 183:   *'If you . . . your hand.'* Bob Proctor, X, 24 Jul 2020. <https://twitter. com/bobproctorLIVE/status/1286663699244224514>

p. 191:   *'You are . . . with most.'* Tim Ferriss, *The 4-Hour Work Week*, 2007.

p. 208:   *'Even fallen . . . us up.'* Mark Neop, *The Book of Awakening*, 1999.

p. 229:   *'Today is . . . about yesterday.'* Dale Carnegie, *How to Stop Worrying and Start Living*, 1944.

p. 253:   *'You're my . . . my everything.'* 'You're the First, the Last, My Everything', performed and produced by Barry White, lyrics by Barry White, Tony Sepe and Peter Radcliffe, 1974.

Charity Resources

Charities and organisations to support you, or who you can support:

Bowel Cancer UK – www.bowelcanceruk.org.uk

Cancer research UK – www.cancerresearchuk.org

Macmillan cancer support – www.macmillan.org.uk

Colostomy UK – www.colostomyuk.org

Bowelbabe Fund – www.bowelbabe.org

Bobby Moore Fund –www.cancerresearchuk.org/get-involved/bobby-moore-fund

Guts UK! – www.gutscharity.org.uk

A Bear Named Buttony – www.buttonybear.com

Southport & Ormskirk Hospitals Charity – www.sohcharity.org

Ataxia UK – www.ataxia.org.uk

Attitude Magazine Foundation – www.attitudemagazinefoundation.com

Heads Together – www.headstogether.org.uk

And, while not a charity, a special mention to the fantastic NO BUTTS campaign, presented by Lorraine Kelly and the wonderful team at ITV's Lorraine (more information on www.itv.com/lorraine).

Listen to the Soundtrack of *Personal Best*

I hope you enjoy listening along to my *Personal Best* playlist!

Notes

I hope you've enjoyed reading *Personal Best* as much as I have writing it. Thank you for coming on this journey with me! I've left space here for you to jot down your thoughts and ideas in response, or maybe to write down your own playlist! I'd love it if you tagged me on Instagram if you share anything on social media (@adeleroberts).

Love,

Adele ♥

....
....
....
....
....
....
....
....
....
....
....
....
....
....
....
....
....
....
....
....
....
....
....
....
....
....
....
....
....
....

PERSONAL BEST

NOTES

PERSONAL BEST

262

NOTES

NOTES

PERSONAL BEST

266